A History of the Electric Locomotive

Also by F. J. G. Haut:
History of the Electric Locomotive, Vol. 1
Geschichte der Elektr. Triebfahrzeuge, Vol. 1 & 2
The Early History of the Electric Locomotive
Electric Motive Power
The Mechanical Layout of C-C & B-B-B Electric Locomotives
Electric Locomotive Design
The Centenary of Electric Traction
Technical & Railway Relics
Railway Electrification with 50 Cycle A.C.
Historia Lokomotiwy Elektrycinej
The Centenary of the Semmering Railway & its Locomotives
The Crossing of the Alps by Rail
Electric Locomotives of the World
Electrification Manchester—Sheffield
Some Notes About the Little Railways of Europe
Along the Right Lines (Locomotive Power Transmission
    Designs)
The Main Line Electric Locomotive
Die Lokomotiven in Gross–Britannien, 1940–50
History of Locomotive Power Transmission
The Steam Railcar
Der Dampftriebwagen
The Pictorial History of the Electric Locomotive

A History of the Electric Locomotive, Volume 2

F. J. G. Haut

San Diego • New York
A. S. Barnes & Company, Inc.
In London:
The Tantivy Press

First Edition
Manufactured in the United States of America

For information write to:
A.S. Barnes & Company, Inc.
P.O. Box 3051
La Jolla, California 92038

The Tantivy Press
Magdalen House
136–148 Tooley Street
London, SE1 2TT, England

Library of Congress Cataloging in Publication Data (Revised)
Haut, F   J   G
    The pictorial history of electric locomotives.

    First published in 1969 under title: The history of the electric
locomotive.
    Vol. 2 has title: History of the electric locomotive.
    Bibliography: v. 1, p. ; v. 2, p.
    1. Electric locomotives—History. I. Title. II. Title:
History of the electric locomotive.
TF975.H3   1969b   625.2′63′09   76-103871
ISBN 0-498-02466-0

1 2 3 4 5 6 7 8 9   84 83 82 81

Contents

Preface

After the considerable success of my earlier publication, *History of the Electric Locomotive*, which so far has appeared in four editions (in the U.S.A., England, Switzerland [German edition], and Poland) and is being translated into other languages, I was advised to describe the history of the "other half" of electric traction vehicles, namely the motor coach and motorcoach train, also called the railcar or interurban. These vehicles and their history have found even less attention than the electric locomotive and its history.

The task of describing the electric motor coach and its history is possibly even more difficult than the electric locomotive history, because the many steps in the development of the electric motor coach took place over 70 years in most countries of the industrial world. The choice of typical examples and the review of inventions and designs had to be not only highly selective but restricted to mainline motor coaches and trains; only where it was historically essential were tram-like efforts considered. Consequently, I have purposely left out the history of the tram, suburban, and metropolitan railways. These might possibly form the subject of a third and final volume.

The advice and help of the publishers in writing this book were of great value; in addition, many railway lines, manufacturing companies, and museums contributed generously by providing required information and illustrations.

Purley, England

The Author

Introduction

A complete history of electric traction so far has not been written. The only attempts were those of F. X. Saurau in Vienna and the publications and lectures of the author. The reasons for this apparent failure are the lack of reliable sources of information and, of course, the fact that electric traction is younger than steam and never has had as many adherents and admirers. However, regional histories, especially in Switzerland, exist and are well documented.

A history of electric traction vehicles divides logically into three groups: locomotives, single motor coaches, and motorcoach trains. Early electric locomotives followed steam locomotive designs, with early steam engines and boilers replaced by electric motors. The second group, the single motor coach, was developed from the horse and steam tram, where again the "moving power" was substituted by an electric motor. The third group, the motorcoach train, is entirely an electric railway development, although there were, of course, steam motor coaches that hauled one or two trailers.

The most remarkable and essential developments of suburban and express services rest entirely on the mounting of electric motors under the motor coach frame, an innovation that resulted in fast, efficient, and frequent commuter services. In addition to the motors, other electrical installations are mounted underframe, such as resistances and the ingenious invention of F. J. Sprague, multiple-unit control. This device from the start enabled an operator to control all motors of a train from one or more positions.

This history of the single motor coach and the motorcoach train first describes the pioneering efforts; developments are in chronological order and are arranged by country. In addition, there is a short history of the industrial and mining locomotive, followed by short biographies of some of the engineers and inventors who created this new field of technical development. As mentioned in the Preface, the history of the motor coach proved even more difficult to cover than that of the locomotive, because original documents are usually no longer in existence. The historian consequently was forced to use material and information from second-hand sources. The indulgence of the reader is therefore requested if dimensions, dates, and other information are uncertain or missing. The author would be most grateful for any information readers might be able to supply that could be used in a later edition.

This recorded history of electric traction vehicles hopefully contributes a better understanding and appreciation of this vital and significant transportation mode to readers, whether they be railwaymen or hobbyists.

List of Abbreviations

(A) Manufacturing Companies

G.E.C.—General Electric Co. of U.S.A.

G.E.C.—General Electric Co. Ltd. of England.

B.T.H.—British Thomson–Houston Co. Ltd., England.

E.E.C.—English Electric Co. Ltd., England.

METRO-VICK.—Metropolitan Vickers Electrical Co. Ltd., England.

SSH or SIEMENS—2 Firms:
Siemens & Halske A.G., Germany.
Siemens-Schuckert A.G., Germany.

A.E.G.—Allgemeine Elektrizitats-Gesellschaft, Germany.

UNION E.J.—Union Elektrizitats-Gesellschaft, Germany.

ELIN.—Elin A.G., Austria.

BBC.—Brown, Boveri & Co. Ltd., Switzerland.

MFO—Maschinen Fabrik Oerlikon, Switzerland.

Oe B.B.C.—Austrian Brown, Boveri Ltd., Austria.

SAAS—Societé Anonyme des Atéliers de Sécheron, Switzerland.

SLM—Swiss Locomotive & Machine Works, Switzerland.

(B) Railway Companies

L.N.E.R.—London & North Eastern Railway, England.

S.R.—Southern Railway, England.

L.M.S.—London, Midland & Scottish Railway, England.

Oe. B.B.—Austrian Federal Railways.

S.B.B.—Swiss Federal Railways.

BLS.—Berne-Lotschberg-Simplon Railway, Switzerland.

F.S.—Italian State Railways.

SJ—Swedish State Railways.

SNCF—French State Railways.

DR—German State Railways. (Pre-1945 and also from 1945 East German Railways.)

DB—German Federal Railways. (Western Germany)

SNCB—Belgian State Railways.

NS—Dutch State Railways.

Part 1

History of the Electric Motor Coach

Early Experiments: 1840–79, and Pioneering Efforts: 1879–1914*

In its infancy, electric railway traction and its vehicles had a very modest start, with the earliest inventions occurring when steam traction was contemporary. Without any notable breakthroughs, the unstable electrical industry tried to find new fields of activity.

But some early electric rail innovations did find merit. The experiments of Thomas Davenport of Vermont started in about 1835, resulting in several electrical working models. It was the Scotsman Davidson who showed his electrically driven motor coach in 1842 at a time when the steam locomotive was in no way at the limits of its capabilities.

Only when steam had reached its limits in terms of cost, availability, power output, and speed did electric traction begin to replace this venerable transport mode. This was the case from about 1900 to 1910, when growing towns needed efficient and frequent suburban and commuter services. Moreover, the crossing of the Alps and American mountain ranges, with their long tunnels and heavy gradients, very quickly demonstrated the limitations of steam traction.

In 1847, Lilley and Cotton, as well as M. G. Farmer, displayed small vehicles in America that created a rotating motion with the aid of batteries and magnetic repulsion. Similar efforts were made by Hall and Page in 1851, also in the United States. Between 1860 and 1866, the dynamo-electric machine, as it was called, was developed. Its first real success was Werner von Siemens's famous exhibition locomotive and train of 1879, which is preserved in the Technical Museum in Munich. Further pioneering efforts were made by Thomas A. Edison, Stephen D. Field, Van Depoele, and Leo Daft.

The Berlin–Lichterfelde Experiments in Germany

In 1881, the first public electric railway—the tramway line from the Berlin railway station at Lichterfelde to Gross–Lichterfelde—was opened. This standard-gauge line, built by the firm of Siemens, had current supplied through both running rails. Rail-ends were connected, wheels had insulated wooden discs, and current was collected by sliding shoes on the tires. Power transmission from motor to driving axle was made through a rope drive, and reversing was accomplished through reversal of the motor. Later, an overhead current supply was introduced and the current was collected by bow collectors.

*Several developments that took place after 1914 also are included.

Berlin–Lichterfelde experiments, with plus and minus running rail, one motor, 7.4 kw, 180-v.

Vehicle with bow collector, 1890.

The German Experiments Berlin–Wannsee–Zehlendorf and Berlin–Gross Lichterfelde Ost

Between 1901 and 1903, the firm of Siemens and Halske carried out experiments that decidedly showed that single-phase traction could be used for railway purposes and that they satisfactorily solved the problem of pole-changing and motor cooling. The tests were conducted on the Berlin–Wannsee–Zehlendorf line, a distance of about 12 km. At the same time, the American Lamme solved the problem of A.C. motors by inserting resistances into the commutator connections, and the firm of Union E.G. succeeded in producing by means of a shunt a simple collector-motor, which was a pure repulsion-induction motor. The ideas belonged to two engineers from Vienna, Austria, Winter and Friedrich Eichberg (see biography of the latter), and their design permitted the use of higher voltages. The motor behaved like a D.C. motor; it ran at reduced speed as the load increased, which meant that speed regulation and starting could be accomplished easily and efficiently. The motor was connected to a step-transformer for safe and simple speed regulation.

Experimental train of the Wannseebahn.

AEG-Winter-Eichberg 25 Hz repulsion motor, 750-v, 20 hp, used
for the Blankenese–Ohlsdorf–Hamburg Line and for the London,
Brighton, and South Coast Railway.

Rotor for the Winter–Eichberg motor.

Experimental train for Niederschoeneweide–Spindlersfeld.

Niederschoeneweide–Spindlersfeld Line, Germany

In 1903, the Prussian State Railways started experiments on this line using single-phase alternating current (A.C.) for mainline traction. A compensated repulsion-induction motor developed by AEG was used on 220-ton trains with 30 axles and a motor coach at each end. Current was supplied through a conductor rail and taken to the train by sliding contact-shoes; return current was conducted through the running rails.

Following these experiments came the introduction of high-tension current on the Berlin–Gross–Lichterfelde Ost line, also in 1903. These experiments were more successful than those of the Wannsee–Bahn, since a far denser traffic could be accommodated. The most important result of these tests was the building in 1907 of the 28-km-long Suburban Line from Cologne to Bonn (see later chapter on this line). The line had 1,000-volt (v) tension in open country and 500-v within the city areas. With the application of the so-called "3-wire-system" and a 2-pole overhead line, 2 x 750-v tension could be attained.

In 1904, two motor coaches were ordered for the Spindlersfeld experiments, each having two 100-horsepower (hp) Winter-Eichberg motors with the following main dimensions: motor speed 800 revolutions per minute (rpm); transmission ratio, 1:4.26; wheel diameter, 1,000 mm; weight of motors with gearboxes, 2,360 kg. The tare-weight of each motor coach was 47.2 tons. The vehicles were to run under 6,000-v tension and use overhead current supply. In 1905, more vehicles were ordered that had two 6-pole 30-hp Winter-Eichberg motors which could run either under 550-v 40-cycles A.C. or 250/270-v D.C. in series connection. All installations were supplied by AEG.

The experiments were continued by the Prussian State Railways in 1906 on the Oranienburg Ring Railway, 1.76 km long, whereby A.C. of the 1-phase type, 600-v tension, and 25-cycle frequency was used. Two motor coaches from the Niederschoeneweide experiments and an AEG-built 58-ton locomotive with 3 x 350-hp motors were employed in the experiments.

The Brighton Beach Railway, England

One-hour distant from London, the resort of Brighton is famous for its little electric railway that started work in 1883 and is in full use today. The line, which uses motor coaches, was designed and built by Brighton's electrical engineer, Magnus Volk. Originally 2-foot gauge (about 51 cm), the railway was later widened to 2-feet, 8½ inches (about 70 cm), and was constructed 3 km long. A third rail supplied current of 50-v D.C. There are two types of vehicles, one closed for winter traffic, and the other, with open sides, called "toast-racks," for summer traffic. The drivers' positions are in the open.

Winter vehicle of the Brighton Beach Railway by Magnus Volk (England), 1883.

Motor coach and trailer of the Giant's Causeway Railway, Northern Ireland, about 1890.

The Giant's Causeway Railway in Northern Ireland

This little railway in the Antrim province of Northern Ireland ran from Portrush to Bushmills (about 9 kilometers distant) and to the Giant's Causeway, a well-known tourist attraction. The railway was opened in 1883, the firm of Siemens Brothers of London supplying the electrical equipment by which the celebrated engineer Edward Hopkinson carried out the designs. Originally the railway was to follow the Berlin Exhibition Railway and the Lichterfelde experiments and was to use a two-rail system with insulated rails and wheels with wooden discs. The system worked well in dry weather, but damp rails led to considerable current losses. Eventually a third

rail was laid, whereby a sliding contact acted as current collector. The vehicle had two such current collectors, one at each end of the motor coach. The line, which had a three-foot gauge (910 mm), started work with two motor coaches, three trailers, and two steam trams for the town, where it was considered unsafe to use electric rails. Work was carried out under the direction of William A. Traill (see biography), whose enthusiasm brought success to the enterprise. Motor coaches had 5-hp output to move the 4-ton vehicles with 20 passengers. A water power station that produced 250-v D.C. was erected with two vertical turbines that drove the twin-pole generators; each turbine's output was about 90 hp. All installations worked satisfactorily for more than

60 years, and in 1887 another section was opened that linked the railway with the actual causeway. In 1900, the system was changed to an overhead catenary. Although the railway survived both world wars, the local authority was not prepared to renew the fixed installations and the line was closed in 1950.

The vehicles are of great interest, but detailed information is difficult to obtain because the railway did not keep exact records. The first electric motor coaches had a 2-pole Siemens motor of about 4 hp that was mounted under the coach frame; it drove the axle by a chain. Reversal of direction was carried out by reversal of the rotor brushes. The vehicles had hand brakes and speeds of 18 km/h were reached. Speed could be adjusted by means of a kind of centrifugal control. The vehicles were very well equipped, having paneled walls, lantern roof, and open-end platforms. Some of the summer vehicles had open sidewalls ("toast-racks"). The motor coaches were 15 feet long, and the wheel base was 6 feet, 6 inches. When the line closed down in 1950, it owned 6 motor coaches and 13 trailers. Today, in the changed climate of industrial archaeology, the railway probably would have been preserved both as a unique technical relic and tourist attraction.

Moedling–Hinterbruehl, Austria

One of the first European railway electrification projects was this meter-gauge line between two small resorts near Vienna. The line belonged to the Austrian Southern Railway and was built by Siemens and Halske. It opened in 1883, was 4.4 km long, and used 500-v D.C. from a 2-pole catenary. The positive and negative line consisted of steel tubes, slotted underneath. Inside the tubes moved brass sliding shoes that acted as current collectors; these were trailed by a rope from the motor coach. The entire construction was hung between steel masts in a kind of catenary suspension. In 1903, bow collectors were introduced.

The Akron-Cleveland Railroad, U.S.A.

In 1884, two American engineers, E. M. Bentley and W. H. Knight, built an electric railway from Akron to Cleveland, 3 kilometers distant. Current was supplied to the vehicles by a kind of channel wherein ran a sliding shoe that was connected by a sliding cable to the vehicle. The motor, mounted between the axles, drove them by a rope-drive. It was probably the first attempt to use a series-connected motor for rail purposes. One of these motors was clearly an early nose-suspended type.

The Pier Railway at Southend near London

One of the earliest pier railways was opened in 1883 at Southend near London, first with horse-drawn vehicles that later were steam-driven and finally electrified in 1889. The firm of Crompton carried out the changeover to electric traction. At first the railway had only one vehicle and one pair of rails, and its current was 200-v D.C. By 1902, however, there were 16 vehicles (four trains with four coaches each) and a central bypass station. In the same year, voltage was increased to 500. The railway has a 3-feet 6-inch gauge (1,080 mm) and a third-rail current system. In 1929, the line was again modernized and was rebuilt as a two-line system equipped with color-light signals. Thirty-two new vehicles were suppled by Falcon of Loughborough. Seven-coach trains operate with a motor coach in the center of the train, each motor coach having two 27-hp motors supplied by BTH. The outer trailers have cabs, so-called driving trailers, and the coaches have open sidewalls. Each train has a capacity of 250 passengers, and in the summer season four such trains are in constant use. During World War II the line was closed but was re-opened in 1945. By 1946, it was moving 650,000 passengers per month.

The Experiments of Van Depoele on the Minneapolis, Lyndale, and Minnetonka Railroads, U.S.A.

Van Depoele, one of the pioneer workers on electric railways, in 1881 opened a small electric railway in Minneapolis because the town authorities had refused to sanction a steam tram within the town area. Van Depoele built a 2-axle open vehicle that contained a 2-pole 20-hp Weston motor that drove one axle by a chain drive. Current collection was by pole rod, which hauled a little wagon, running on top of the 2-wire copper catenary. The return current went through the running rails. The line was about

Vehicle No. 9 for above line changed to overhead catenary in about 1909.

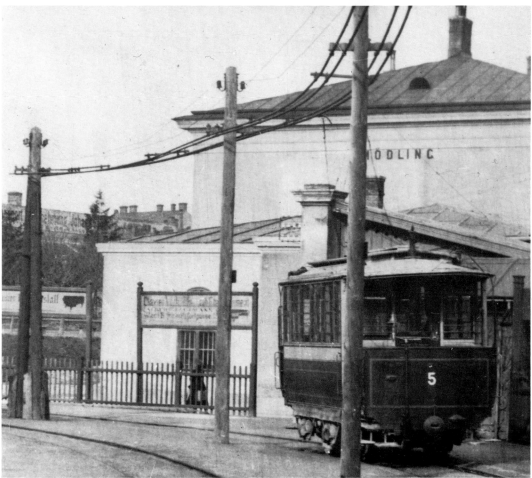

Motor coach and rigid overhead line for Moedling–Hinterbruehl, near Vienna, Austria, 1883.

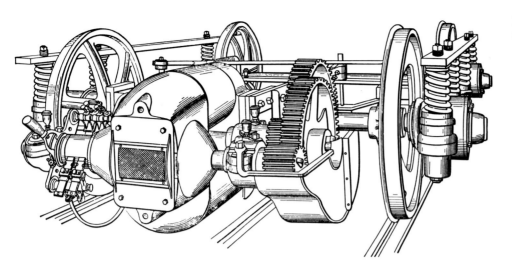

Bentley and Knight early U.S. nose-suspended motor, 1885.

2½ km long and the motor coach, which took an unspecified number of passengers, hauled four 10-ton trailers, for a total weight of about 60 tons. The primitive installation worked very well, but because it caused considerable and expensive maintenance, the line was closed in 1904.

The "Interurban" Railroads of the U.S.A.

The development of these unique "interurban" transport systems form an important part of both American railway history and electric traction.

The interurbans started as steam lines and were superceded after their electrified existence by ever-growing automobile traffic. Development of automobile transportation continued until the 1970s, when road traffic with its congestion, accidents, and increase costs led to the beginning of a reversal of these trends.

Originally, the main attraction of interurban lines was their easy accessibility and comfort as compared to main lines. Development started in about 1890 and reached its zenith in 1910 to 1912; a decline began after 1918 and by 1938 only a few lines were left; by 1970 hardly anything existed of this once gigantic transport system.

In the 1880s, as towns grew ever bigger, the horse-tram was still the mainstay of public transport. When it became unsuitable and unsatisfactory, the electric streetcar and railway were its natural successors.

The efforts of the various early pioneers are certainly part of the history of the electric streetcar.

One of the leading personalities was F. J. Sprague, whose first great success was the electric railway system in Richmond, Virginia, followed by similar works in other areas of America and Europe. Soon the town streetcars were extended into suburbs and neighboring towns. Vehicles got heavier, but since the lines led along public highways, they were much easier to reach than ordinary railway main lines and their stations. An American source gives the following excellent definition of an interurban:

Electric traction, mainly passenger services, mainly heavy (railway-like) vehicles (as opposed to tramway cars) and rails along the main roads within towns and on proper railway tracks outside towns.

The first interurban might well have been the Giant's Causeway Electric Tramway in Ireland, which was built in 1889 by Siemens and mentioned earlier. The first American line was the Newark and Granville Street Railway in Ohio, which was opened in 1889–1890. Various smaller systems followed in Ohio, where the well-to-do outlying villages and suburbs needed good connections with their main towns. Such systems, created by enterprising engineers, appeared in Ohio and Detroit, Michigan. One syndicate, the Everett-More group, had no less than 2,500 kilometers of line in service in 1902; of course, many were ill-planned and never showed reasonable results and profits.

By 1903, the first boom was at an end, but building of lines continued and many systems were linked together. For example, the Ohio Electric had a 350-km-long main line in 1918 from Cincinnati to Toledo; express trains took five and a half hours to

New York, New Haven & Hartford Railroad's D.C. motorcoach train of 1894–1908 for the Nantasket Beach Line.

Three-coach train of the Galveston–Houston, Texas, interurban railroad, painted in blue and white and covering 80 kilometers in 75 minutes.

traverse the 270-km-long main section from Dayton to Toledo. The Ohio Electric had become big business: in 1909 it moved 23 million passengers, had 1,067 kilometers of line, and used 320 motor coaches and 110 trailers. But in 1907 a new financial crisis came and many lines were never completed. After 1908 only 8,000 kilometers of the line was built, the last in 1927.

As far as the technical principles of the interurbans are concerned, it was always planned to use motor coaches, with or without trailers, because the primitively constructed track needed heavy and powerful vehicles. Often, gradients reached 80‰ since the lines avoided all civil engineering work and were laid simply along the road both in and out of towns or sometimes outside of towns on their own tracks. This practice caused obvious problems and accidents, especially because no supervising authority existed, gauges even varied, and nobody thought of linking the various competing systems together. Electrically, the lines used mostly 500 to 750-v D.C. and some had conductor rails.

The 1-phase A.C. railways were supplied primarily by Westinghouse and used 3,300 or 6,000-v A.C., reducing this within town areas to 500/600-v; later, most of the lines were rebuilt to use 1,200/1,500-v D.C.

Early traction vehicles were similar to heavy streetcars with wooden bodies and open sides for summer traffic; all were double-bogie vehicles. They carried 32 to 50 passengers, were 12 to 16 meters (m) long, and reached speeds 40 to 60 km/h.

Most of the lines in Ohio and in the whole of the Middle West later developed forms characteristic of heavy U.S. railway coaches. They had a wooden coach body, lantern roof, and were either passenger coaches only or also had a luggage and mail compartment. Coach interiors were luxuriously appointed and exteriors were painted in bright colors, orange becoming especially well known. The heavier vehicles were 15 to 21 meters long.

Several wagonworks specialized in these relatively simple, efficient, and attractively designed vehicles, as for example the firm of Niles and Jewett in Ohio. Production reached its zenith probably in 1912 when no less than 1,245 motor coaches were ordered. Almost all vehicles were fully motorized, with four nose-suspended motors and an hourly output of 50 to 100 hp. The driving installations were very simple. Speed regulation was achieved by insertion of resistances, whereby two motors were connected in parallel. Many of the vehicles had only one front driver's cab and current was collected by pole-trolley.

Sprague was the inventor of the multiple-unit control, which was used on main lines and trains where up to 15 coaches were operated. The bogies were always cast iron and four-wheeled. From 1910

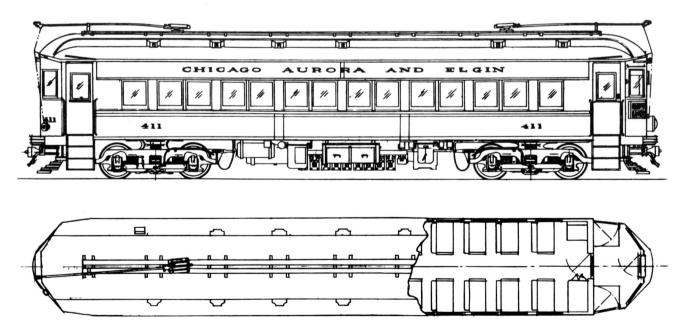

Pullman all-steel coach of the Chicago, Aurora, and Elgin R.R. of 1923. Four 140-hp motors, 600-v D.C., 120 km/h maximum speed.

1902 train of the Chicago, Aurora, and Elgin Railroad, one of 10 with steel frames, wooden coachbodies, and luxurious fittings with paneled walls. This was an important interurban line.

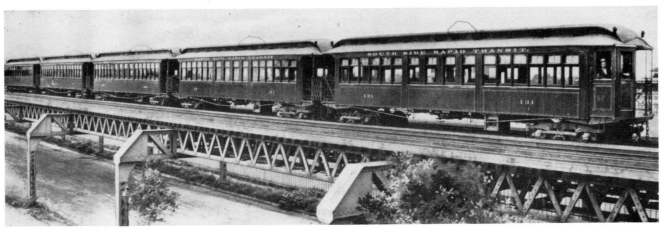

Five-coach train of the Chicago, South Side Elevated R.R. with Sprague's multiple-unit control.

onwards, vehicles with steel bodies were built, and although the maintenance costs decreased, weights increased to up to 57 tons, a heavy load for these poorly laid rail lines.

In the twenties, lightweight vehicles began to appear, weighing 18 to 20 tons. The leading manufacturer was the Cincinnati Car Company, Ltd. One-man control was common. After 1930, very few vehicles were built. An attempt was made in 1941 by the North Shore Line to use modern vehicles called Electroliners, which were four-coach trains for the Chicago–Milwaukee route. They had five 2-axle bogies, were 93,300-mm-long, and were designed as dining, sleeping, and saloon coaches. After World War II, nearly the whole fleet of vehicles was scrapped except for about a dozen coaches that were preserved as museum pieces. In the seventies, however, a resurgence of interest in organized rail traffic

has caused study groups to order test vehicles for suburban railways.

Freight traffic was limited. Mostly Bo-Bo locomotives were used, but freight motor coaches called box cars also were employed. A few lines also used heavy locomotives, such as the $2\text{-}D_0\text{+}D_0\text{-}2$ type of the South Shore Line. There were three such locomotives, each with 6,000-hp output. These 27,400-mm-long locomotives were destined for Russia, but the U.S. authorities forbade their export for military reasons. Similar locomotives were supplied to the Chicago, Milwaukee, and St. Paul Railroad for its Rocky Mountain lines.

The history of the interurban lines easily could fill several books. After an initial success, they declined with the ever-increasing reliance upon the automobile. The Depression of the thirties sealed their fate. Obviously, many of the lines were ill-planned, purely speculative enterprises that were encouraged by an almost total lack of public supervision.

One line, however, lived on and in the end turned into a full-scale mainline railway. The Chicago, South Shore, and South Bend Railroad, also known as the South Shore Line, began operation between Chicago and South Bend in 1909 (144 kilometer distance). In the beginning, 6,000-v, 1-phase A.C. was used on overland sections and 600-v D.C. on town sections. There were two types of current collectors: bow trolleys for D.C. and pantographs for A.C. sections. As the trains went through three towns, current had to be changed five times.

Despite its initial success, the company fell into debt, was declared bankrupt, and was sold in 1925 to the famous (or infamous) Samuel Insull, an early example of the "take-over" man. Under his energetic management, the line was reorganized, 68 new steel vehicles were ordered, and the current was changed to 1,500-v D.C. An agreement with the Illinois Central Railroad assured the connection to Chicago. Success resulted and the line blossomed and made profits, increasing traffic many times, until the

Depression of 1933. Yet the line survived and in the sixties, 20 trains were moved per day in each direction between Chicago and South Bend with speeds up to 140 km/h. Freight traffic also was successfully developed by using locomotive haulage.

The Liverpool Overhead Railway, England

This railway, opened in 1893, is about 10-km-long and is double line throughout. Forty-six vehicles were ordered for this railway, which is the first metropolitan railway in the modern sense that was run electrically. Most of the line runs on cast iron viaducts, about 5–6 m above ground. Originally, there was a central conductor rail and later a side rail. The first vehicles were twin-bogied with the outer axles of each bogie motorized. Eleven two-coach trains, each end having a driver's cab, were ordered, with 57 seats per vehicle. Current used was first 500-v, then 800-v D.C., and wheel diameter was 670 mm. In 1901, 12 three-coach trains were introduced, which increased the capacity of the line considerably. These vehicles were supplied by Dick, Kerr & Company, a forerunner of the English Electric Company.

Liverpool Overhead Railway's 1901 motorcoach train. Supplied by Dick, Kerr & Co., later part of the English Electric Co.

Liverpool Overhead Railway: "sliding shoe" current collector for central current rail as supplied for the original 1893 vehicles.

PAUL B. CORS

Motor coach and summer vehicles ("toast rack") of the Douglas and Laxey Coast Electric Railway of the Isle of Man, Great Britain, supplied by Mather & Platt.

Each train had two end-motor coaches and a non-motorized center coach. The motor coaches each had two 200-hp motors, equipped with series-parallel connections. A further series of vehicles was supplied by English Electric, consisting of 38 motor coaches and 19 trailers with two 75-hp motors per motor coach.

The Electric Lines on the Isle of Man, Great Britain

The Isle of Man in the Irish Sea has two electric railways that are among the earliest pioneers of electric traction and are still in full use, mostly with the original equipment, and in splendid condition. The two railways are the Manx Electric Railway, with a gauge of 3½ feet (1,050 mm), and the Snaefell Railway, with a gauge of 3 feet (915 mm).

The first line is 27-km-long and leads from Douglas to Ramsey. Built in 1893, it originally had 2½ foot gauge (760 mm). The early fate of the line was very mixed because it depended originally on tourist traffic, which badly suffered during war times and depression. After World War II, the line was recognized as a very important tourist attraction, was acquired by the municipalities, and was thoroughly overhauled. The vehicles are of museum importance and are in full use in their original liveries.

From the village of Laxey, Snaefell Railway climbs up the 678 meter-high Snaefell Mountain, the highest elevation on the Isle of Man. This 8-km-long line, opened in 1895, has a "Fell" central friction rail that is used for braking with the aid of friction discs

and shoes since the gradient is no less than 85‰. The firm of G. F. Milnes supplied six vehicles, all 4-axled and with 48 seats. Each axle is motorized with an 85-hp motor and there are two bow collectors.

The Orbe–Chavornay Railway, Switzerland

In 1894, the little town of Orbe was connected by rail with Chavornay, a station on the Lausanne–Neufchatel Line (Simplon–Jura), a distance of 4 kilometers. This was the first standard-gauge electric railway in Switzerland. The work was carried out by the firm of Cie de l'Industrie et Mécanique in Geneva under the direction of the famous engineer

Motor coach of the Snaefell Mountain Railways, Isle of Man, built by Mather & Platt of Manchester.

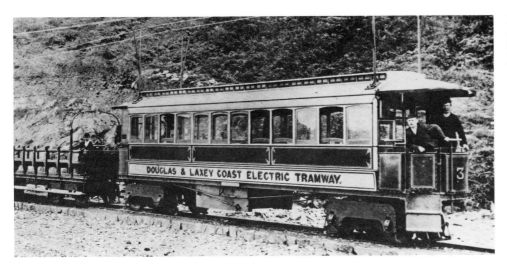

Experimental train with motor coach supplied in 1893 for Douglas and Laxey Coast Electric Railway; still in full use.

Motor coach for the Orbe–Chavornay Railway.

René Thury (see biography). The firm existed until 1918 when it was absorbed by the Sécherôn group in Geneva.

Current used was 660-v D.C., and the rolling stock consisted originally of two passenger motor coaches and one freight motor coach. The vehicles had two motors of 30 hp each and 300 rpm; they could haul a trailing load of 30 tons and were 9.90 m and 7.40 m long, respectively. One of the vehicles was later reconstructed, and between 1915 and 1928 four additional vehicles were ordered. (Table 1 gives details of the vehicles and their main dimensions.)

In the 1920s, the trolley current collectors were replaced by bow collectors and by pantographs in 1956. Before this standard-gauge line, there existed the meter-gauge line, Geneva–Veyrier, which received a 2-axle motor coach in 1891. The vehicles, type Ce 2/2–18, were equipped for 500-v D.C. and had two 2.5-hp motors. The vehicle part was supplied by Geissberger & Company, a forerunner of the Schlieren Wagon Works, while the electrical part was supplied by the Sécherôn group in Geneva.

Table 1
ORBE–CHAVORNAY LINE

Type	Year Built	Length (m)	Wheel-Base (m)	Output (kw)	Builder	Remarks
Ce 2/2	1894	9.90	4.00	2 x 25	SIG/CIEG	
Fe 2/2	1894	7.40	3.00	2 x 25	SIG/CIEG	
CFe 2/2	1895	9.90	4.00	2 x 25	SIG/CIEG	Ex No 1
BDe 4/4	1915	15.78	11.84	4 x 30	SWS/MFO	
BDe 4/4	1920	15.78	11.84	4 x 30	SWS/MFO	
De 2/2	1902 (28)	9.02	3.00	2 x 28	SWS/MFO	
De 2/2	1921	10.70	5.00	2 x 44	SWS/MFO	

The Rack Railway Barmen–Thoelleturm, Germany

In 1894, the firm of Siemens built the first electric rack railway leading from Barmen to Thoelleturm. In this system, the energy of the trains running downhill was used for current-regeneration by using shunt-wound motors and the dynamo effect was used for braking.

The 23.6-km-long line, with a rack section of 1.6 km, had meter-gauge and maximum gradients of 50‰ (adhesion) and 184‰ (rack). Current used was 550-v D.C., supplied through a single-pole catenary. There were 2- and 4-axled motor coaches, and, in all, the railway owned 31 vehicles, of which eight were for the rack section. Maximum speed was 20 km/h and, on the rack section, 10 km/h. The railway was broken up in 1959.

Motor coach for the Barmen Rack Railway, built by Siemens (W. Germany).

Motor coach for the Lugano–Tesserete Line, Switzerland, supplied in 1909 by Brown, Boveri, & Cie.

The Railways in and around Lugano, Switzerland

Lugano is one of the most important towns of the Canton of Tessin (Ticino) in Switzerland. It has a very active local transport system that in itself is almost a miniature history of electric traction. For this reason the whole system is described at length and all its components are shown in detail.

Not only has the town long been a well-known and frequented tourist center but an important stop of the Gotthard line. With its many suburbs and scenic attractions, it forms a natural tourist paradise; in addition, it contains substantial industries and enterprises. The old part of Lugano is very steep and has many narrow streets.

One of the first tram lines in Europe was built in Lugano, which disappeared in due course and was replaced by trolley-buses. In addition, two cable-hauled railways connect the old town with one of its suburbs and the railway station lying high above the lake. Connecting Lugano with its surrounding districts are several interurbans, whose details are listed in Table 2.

There are also two cable-railways leading up the Monte Bré and San Salvatore hills. Lugano's streetcars, with their 350-v, 3-phase current system, played an important step in the development of electric traction. Opened in 1896, the streetcar system, as already mentioned, used 350-v, 3-phase A.C. and was rebuilt in 1910 for 500-v D.C. The electrical installations were supplied by Brown-Boveri and followed the ideas of one of its founders, Charles Brown (see biography). The 12-pole, 3-phase motors produced 20 hp, worked at 42 cycles frequency, and with gears weighed 700 kilograms (kg) or an amazing 35 kg/hp. Three-phase current operation was chosen because a nearby power station supplied this current to the town of Lugano. The system worked satisfactorily and was used later for the Engelberg, Jungfrau, and Gornergrat lines (discussed later).

Table 2
INTERURBANS AROUND LUGANO

Line	Year Opened	Year Closed	Length (km)	Max. Grad. (%)	Gauge	Current
Lugano–Tesserete	1909	1967	8	60	meter	1,000-v D.C.
Lugano–Cadro–Dino	1911	1970	8	40	meter	1,000-v D.C.
Lugano–Ponte Tresa	1912	————	12	30	meter	1,150-v D.C.

Motor coach for Lugano–Ponte Tresa, series BCe 4/4 of 1912.

The firm of Ganz in Budapest undertook similar experiments at the same time. A second line was opened in 1905, but in 1910 the system was renewed with 500-v D.C. and a tramline was built between the town and the main station. In 1959, the entire system was closed down and replaced by trolley-busses. The tramway started operations with four single-motor (20 hp), 2-axle motor coaches for 24 passengers each and 15 km/h speed. These vehicles were supplied by Herbrand in Cologne. In 1910, motor coach types Ce 2/2 appeared and later came partly to the Lugano-Cadro–Dino Line for the La Santa suburban section.

In addition to the main data mentioned above for interurban lines, the Lugano–Cadro–Dino Line initially ordered four 2-axle vehicles from SWS and Alioth, type CFe 2/2, with 2-axle trailers. The motor coaches had two 65-hp motors. In 1914, Brown-Boveri supplied another motor coach, the Ce 2/2, with 2-axles and two 27-hp motors. This railway was already closely linked to the Lugano tram system.

Between 1943 and 1948, the existing motor parts were rebuilt to 3-axle SLM-types. In 1913, one of the rebuilt 3-phase motor coaches of the Lugano tram (Ce 2/2–6), built by SWS/BBC, was in service for awhile. In 1941, the line acquired a motor coach of the Biel–Meinisberg Line (Ce 4/4–10) that had been built in 1937 by SIG/BBC; in 1955 it added a new construction, Be 4/4. In 1970, the line closed down.

The second interurban, the Lugano–Ponte Tresa Railway, opened in 1912, is 12-km-long, has meter-gauge, and uses 1,000-v D.C. current supply. The railway serves the district of Malcantone. The first order, from SWS/Alioth, was for three motor coaches, type BCe 4/4 1–3. These had four 62-hp motors and were in use until 1968. Between 1952–58 there followed ABe 4/4, 4 and 5, supplied by SWS/Sécheron with 31-ton tare weight and four 83-hp motors.

To modernize the railway with up-to-date innovations in suburban transport, the railway in 1968 ordered three new articulated train sets which

Standing cable railways of Lugano, leading to the upper part of the town and the scenic hills of San Salvatore and Monte Bré.

can haul up to three trailers and accommodate 332 passengers. Their weight is 42 tons and there are four 122-hp motors. In 1968, a new fixed timetable was started with 30-minute train frequencies, thus reducing the duration of the journey between Lugano and Ponte Tresa from 27 to 22 minutes. Vehicles No. 4 and 5 are used for freight and slow passenger services, while No. 3 is used as a service and reserve vehicle. The renewal of this narrow-gauge line is a good example of how such lines can become an important part of a well-planned, integrated transport system, avoiding the use of imported costly fuels and reducing the burden on road traffic.

The third narrow-gauge line, Lugano–Tesserete, was opened in 1909, was 8-km-long and used 1,000-v D.C. Originally, the line had three motor coaches, type BCFe 4/4, with two 2-axle bogies; speed was 20 km/h. Other main dimensions were: weight in working order, 23 tons; length, 15,110 mm; wheelbase, 11,000 mm; bogie wheelbase, 2,000 mm; wheel diameters, 800 mm; four motors of 45 hp. Motor regulation permitted two groups in series and parallel connection with controlled resistances. Gear ratio was 1:4.5 and the vehicles had bow collectors. The electrical installations were supplied by Alioth. The railway was successful until 1967, when it was closed down because of the prohibitive costs of bridge and viaduct renewal.

In addition, there are in Lugano two short cable-hauled railways, which, as previously mentioned, link the lakeside town with its higher suburbs and the main station. The first was built in 1881 as a water-ballast line and later was rebuilt for electric traction. The 231-m line, with 48-passenger capacity vehicles, covers a difference in height of 53 m with maximum gradients of 250 percent (per mille).

Furthermore, there are two, larger, cable-hauled railways that go up the San Salvatore and Monte Bré mountains. The Monte Bré is built in two sections, the lower section opening in 1908 and the upper one in 1912. The two sections are 208 m and 1,413 m long and rise 96 and 520 m, respectively. The two sections avoid using too long a cable; in addition, the lower section serves a densely populated suburb (Suvigliano) and has a far denser traffic than the upper section. On the first section, vehicles carry 42 passengers, and on the second section, modern lightweight vehicles take 70 passengers. The railway has meter-gauge and gradients of 600 and 470‰. Since its reconstruction, the railway is remote-controlled, whereby one of the pantographs receives the traction current while the other one connects electrically with the remote-control station.

The railway up the San Salvatore mountain was opened in 1890, also in two sections, but with a single cable. The vehicles were supplied by Bell of Kriens/Lucerne and were replaced in 1954 by new vehicles. The original coaches had wooden bodies and a riveted steel frame; the modern ones are built in stressed lightweight construction with a modern braking system. The lengths of the sections are 828 m and 830 m, with gradients of 380 and 600‰. Traveling time is 15 minutes, and the 78-passenger vehicles travel at 9 km/h.

Motor coach ABDe 4/44 and 5 for Lugano–Ponte Tresa, built 1952–58.

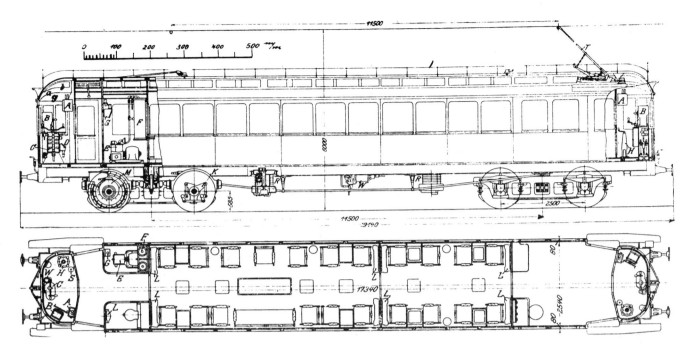

F = Air chamber   G = Auto circuit breaker of E.   T = Reel receiver   R = Fluid resistance   M = Motor   K = Coupling between motor and axle
E = Compressor   C = Current reverse and cutoff of drive   A = Safety   B = Main circuit breaker   D = Motor cutout switch
W = Westinghouse brake

Motor coach of the Valtellina or Weltlin Railway.

The work of Ganz & Co. of Budapest, Hungary: The Weltlin or Valtellina Railway

The firm of Ganz & Company had already produced electrical equipment for several years when in 1896 it erected a substantial factory in Budapest, thereby founding the firm of Ganz E.G. In the same year the firm had built within its own factory yard a meter-gauge railway for test purposes, using 500-v 2-phase A.C. In 1899, a test-line followed at Alt–Ofen Isle in Budapest that was 1.5-km-long and used 3,000-v 3-phase A.C. with a small 2-axle locomotive. Two

years later, the firm supplied one of the earliest electric mining locomotives (Bleiberg).

In 1902, Ganz & Company electrified the Welt-lin, or Valtellina, Railway, a significant historical event. This line traverses a very beautiful Alpine valley from Lecco to Colico and to Chiavenna and Sondrio, Italy. Current was 3,000-v 3-phase A.C. of 15 Hz and locomotives and motor coaches were proposed. These efforts formed the basis for the later electrification of the Simplon Line. The Weltlin Railway received four types of locomotives, whose details are given in Table 3.

Table 3
WELTLIN OR VALTELLINA RAILWAY

Year supplied	Wheel arrangement	Weight in working order (t)	1-hour motor output (hp)	Driving wheel diameter (mm)
1901	Bo-Bo	46	4 x 225	1,396
1903	1-C-1	62	2 x 450	1,500
1905	1-C-1	62	2 x 1,500	1,500
1907	1-C-1	62	2 x 1,800	1,500

In addition, motor coaches were supplied that had two 2-axle bogies; one of the bogies had a 3,000-v high-tension motor, the other a 300-v cascade-arrangement motor. Output was 250 hp with a 1,140 mm wheel diameter and a 3.8-ton motor weight. Traveling speed was 65 km/h for trains of five to seven coaches and 150-ton weight on gradients of 10‰.

The Budapest Underground Railway

Another pioneering effort was the Budapest underground railway of 1896, constructed by Siemens and Halske and H. Schwieger. The line, built by the cut-and-cover method under the surface of one of the main streets of Budapest—Andrassy Street—is 3.75-km-long and has the very limited tunnel height of 2.75 m. It was the first express underground railway in the world. The railway has standard-gauge, uses 300-v D.C., and for its whole distance it is double-tracked. Of its length, 3.22 kilometers are in tunnel, the remainder at surface level. Maximum gradient is 18.4 percent. The line has 11 stops, including nine underground stations. As conductor rails, running rails are used to form a twin arrangement in the center of the rails. The 20 motor coaches work singly, and each has two driver's cabs and a cranked center part to allow a stepless entry to the floor, which is only 15 cm above platform level. Main dimensions of the vehicles are as follows: total length, 11,120

Motor coach of the cut-and-cover underground railway of Budapest (Hungary) of 1896: two 20 kw/1-hour motors, 320-v D.C., speed 40 km/h.

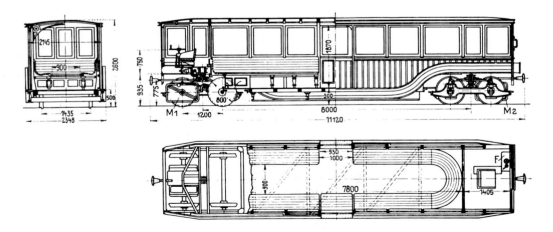

Detailed drawing of the above Budapest underground railway.

mm; distance of bogie centers, 8,000 mm; bogie wheel base, 1,200 mm; wheel diameter, 800 mm. Tare weight is 15 tons and capacity is 40 passengers. Ten vehicles have a 2-pole motor with chain drive and the other ten have a 4-pole motor with a rotor fixed on the outer axles of the bogies. Each coach has two small pantographs. The line is still in full use.

The Vienna–Baden Interurban Express Railway, Austria

The first section of this line was opened in 1898, and in 1907 the total distance of the 30-km-long line was electrified. The railway has standard gauge and uses 550-v D.C. in the town centers and 1-phase A.C. of 15 Hz and 550-v (later 720-v) tension on the open line. Motors were able to run under both currents and the changeover was automatic. Severely damaged in World War II, the line later was rebuilt with 800-v D.C. for the whole length.

The coaches in this railway are in themselves a short history of electric traction vehicles. Original motor coaches were 4-axled with two fully motorized bogies. Nineteen units were ordered with the following main particulars: total weight, 27.5 tons; weight of electrical part, 10.5 tons; length, 13,000 mm; total wheel base, 7,850 mm; bogie wheel base, 1,850 mm; wheel diameter, 850 mm. The 4 x 40-hp D.C./A.C. series-connected motors worked with 275-v and 15

Motor coach train for the Vienna–Baden Interurban Express Railway, 1930.

Train for the Vienna–Baden Interurban Express Railway, Austria.

hertz (Hz). Two motors were thus permanently connected in series; gear ratio was 1:3.2. There were 44 seats and the one-hour tractive effort was 1,100 kg at 40 km/h. Maximum speed was 60 km/h. Later, other modern vehicles were ordered as traffic between Vienna and the popular resort of Baden continued to grow.

The Stansstad–Engelberg Railway, later the Lucerne–Stansstad–Engelberg Railway, and its Vehicles (Switzerland)

This line's purpose was to connect the growing tourist resorts of the Engelberg area with the main lines of Switzerland, a development that took place at the end of the nineteenth century. The 22-km-long line connected the little resort of Engelberg and its famous monastery to Stansstad on the lake of Lucerne and later with Lucerne itself and the Swiss Federal Railways. Opened in 1898, the meter-gauge railway used 800/850-v 3-phase current and 32–33 Hz until the line was rebuilt in 1964. The line had a

mixed rack-and-adhesion system with adhesive gradients of 50‰. While the rack section is 1,400 mm long, it overcomes a difference in height of 292 m and has gradients of 250‰. Riggenbach rack rail was employed, and the practice was for the rack locomotive to push the train upwards. When running downhill, speed was only 5 km/h and the journey over the rack section took 20 minutes.

In 1929, a combined rack-and-adhesion motor coach built by SLM was acquired, which increased traveling speed. The new motor coach could move on the rack section at 8 km/h and on adhesion reach 25 to 40 km/h. The 4-axle motor coach had two driven axles and the following technical details: diameter of adhesion wheels, 665 mm; rack driving wheels, 573 mm; maximum tractive efforts, 3,000 kg (adhesion); 9,000 kg (rack); weight, 29 tons.

The driving bogie was arranged on the valley side and the car had a 36-seat passenger compartment, as well as a mail and luggage compartment. Speed was controlled by an oil-operated gear-drive whereby, with oil pressure, friction discs were connected and disconnected for the various transmission ratios. The rack driving wheel had sprung toothed

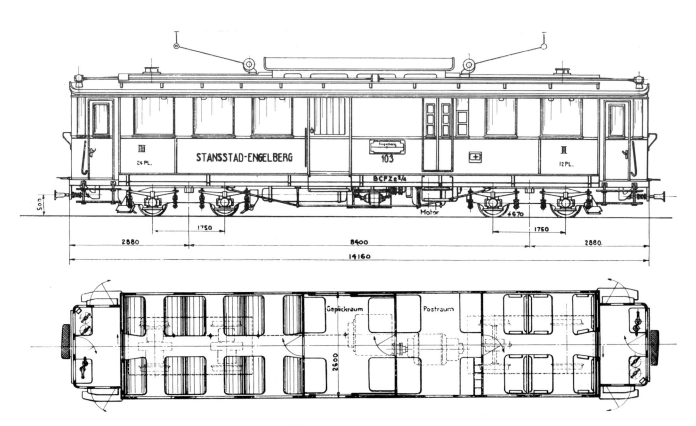

Stansstad–Engelberg Rack and Adhesion Railway; 1929 motor coach.

New three-unit motorcoach train for the modernized Lucerne–Stansstad–Engelberg Line.

rims and the teeth of the rack driving wheel were set to achieve equal power transmission. Other suppliers were BBC for electrical systems and Schlieren for coach equipment.

Traffic increased substantially after World War II, especially through winter sport demands. A large majority decided in a 1959 poll to retain the railway, modernize and extend it to Hergiswil, and link up with the meter-gauge Bruenig Line and Lucerne. The current system was to be changed to 15,000-v 1-phase A.C. of $16\frac{2}{3}$ Hz. Instead of the former 120 minutes, modern train sets were to make the journey in 50 minutes.

In 1964, traffic recommenced with the new train sets, which have two driving coaches at each end and a middle trailer. The trains are designed for 75 km/h in the adhesion section and remain directionally in the same position. The lower-end coach is motorized so that the train is pushed uphill. New vehicles were supplied by SLM, SAAS, BBC, Schindler, Altenrhein, and Neuhausen. Motor coaches (series BDhe 4/4) have 40 seats and a luggage compartment, the driving coach ABt has 20 seats, and the center trailer has 64 seats and a luggage and mail compartment. A mail and luggage van also was ordered. Vehicles are designed according to the latest, state-of-the-art ideas, the motor coaches having pendulum supports by SLM and the tranverse

frame member resting on rubber springs. Hydraulic damping devices reduce vertical movements and oscillation. Each bogie has two axles driven by a motor in a crosswise position. The transmission gear allows for two speeds: 19.5 km/h on rack and 75 km/h on adhesion; it has transmission ratios of 5.2:1 and 17.17:1; electropneumatic disc couplings permit changeover while at speed.

The switchgear arrangements are very interesting and very carefully laid out. There is a master controller that can follow the described programs automatically: zero, advance/adhesion, advance/rail or zero, backwards/adhesion, and backwards/rack. To avoid entering the rack section with the wrong gearing, a device is provided to stop the train without delay. Changeover of gearing can be made only when the motor current is cut off. The electric brake acts automatically at maximum speed and controls maximum load at about 25 km/h (adhesion) or 7 km/h (rack). Besides this delaying action, the electric brake is also functional when moving downhill both on the adhesion and rack sections.

When driving, all four motors are in parallel and the motor voltage is controlled by a low-tension contactor gear, allowing the motors to be used as generators when running downhill. The main switch and earthing switch are fitted on the roof, as are brake resistances, pole change, and extra shunts.

Rack locomotive and adhesion motor coach for Stansstad–Engelberg Railway.

1896 adhesion motor coach for Stansstad–Engelberg Railway.

Early Electric Railways in France

The first railway electrification in France on the Paris–Orléans Line was the 1898 underground section, Paris–Austerlitz–Orsay. It was 4.2-km-long with 11‰ gradient. Current was supplied either through a third rail or an overhead wire and was of 575–600-v tension. Eight locomotives were ordered from Blanc-Misseron following the designs of F. J. Sprague (see biography) and supplied by General Electric. They had the wheel arrangement Bo-Bo and an hourly output of 1,000 hp. The locomotives were designated E1 to E8; in addition, three motor coaches were ordered (E9 to E11) that were destined for the extension to Juvisy (23 kilometers) in 1904. Their weight in working order was 55 tons and they had four 4-pole motors of 125 hp in continuous output. The motor coaches could haul a trailer train of 200 tons with 70 km/h and even reached 100 km/h. To achieve this feat, a motor coach was positioned at each end of the train and multiple-unit control after Sprague/General Electric was used. Until 1907, seven additional motor coaches were ordered in which only the transmission gear was altered, namely from 1:2.23 to 1:3.08.

In the years 1900 to 1902, similar electrifications were carried out by the Ouest Railway (Les Invalides–Les Molineaux–Versailles). For these lines, 10 motor coaches and two motorcoach trains were ordered following the designs of Sprague and Thompson; these were still in full use in the 1950s.

Other main railway companies in France (PLM and Midi) undertook comparable electrification of their suburban lines in the early 1900s. A narrow-gauge railway of the PLM, Le Fayet to Chamonix in the Haute Savoy, was electrified in 1901 with 550-v D.C. and third rail. The 19-km-long line had gradients of 90‰ and used motor coaches, trailers, and also freight cars. Vehicles were 2-axled, weighed 18 to 21 tons, and were 8,600 mm long with a wheel base of 3,500 mm. All axles were driven and the wheels had a diameter of 930 mm, motor output being 65 hp. The two motors of each vehicle were coupled permanently in parallel and had pneumatically controlled resistance regulation of speeds. Transmission ratio was 1:4 and maximum speed was 25 km/h. In 1902, the meter-gauge line of the Midi railways from Villefranche–Vernet–Les Bains to Bourg–Madame in the Cerdagne in the Pyrénées was electrified. (See page 77.)

1901 metal-bodied Sprague multiple-unit trains for Paris–Austerlitz–Versailles.

1,500-v D.C. motor coach of the French Midi Railroad (later transformed for A.C. work).

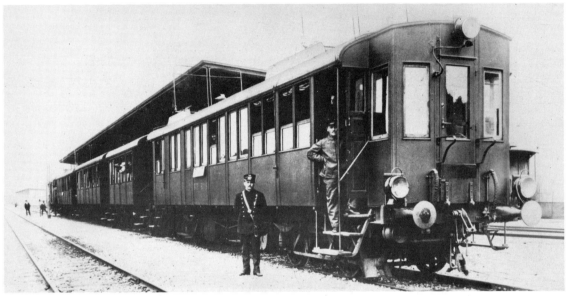

Motor coach of 1899 for the Burgdorf–Thun Railway; first electric main line of Switzerland; 3-phase A.C. current.

The Motor Coaches of the Burgdorf–Thun Railway, later called the Emmental–Burgdorf–Thun Railway, Switzerland

The locomotives of this railway form an important step in locomotive design. This 40.3-kilometer line, opened in 1899, was the first Swiss standard-gauge railway that was electrified from the start.

The railway used 3-phase A.C. of 750-v tension and also had six motor coaches. These were 4-axled, all motorized. There were four 60-hp motors that were nose-suspended and transmitted power by a single gear-drive. Electrical installations, such as resistances, were fixed under the coach frame. There were 66 seats and one trailer of a 60–70-seat capacity could be hauled. Average speed was 36 km/h on 25‰ gradients with a hauled weight of 20 tons. Two trains could be coupled together and thus had a capacity of 280 passengers. Other main dimensions were: bogie wheel base, 2,200 mm; distance of bogie centers, 9,500 mm; total length, 16,300 mm; weight in working order, 32 tons, whereby the electrical part weighed 10 tons.

In 1921, two more motor coaches were introduced consisting of a locomotive part with one motor and two axles and a coupled coach part. Three-phase

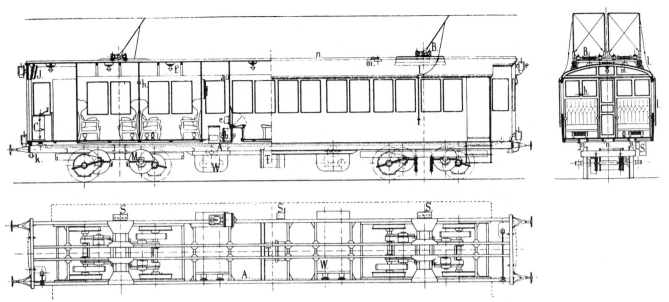

Sectional drawing of Burgdorf–Thun Railway.

Three-phase A.C. motor coach
for Burgdorf–Thun Railway,
delivered in 1921.

services ended in 1932 and were replaced by 1-phase A.C. of 15,000-v and 16⅔ cycles, mainly to link more easily with the interchange stations of the SBB. Traffic developed satisfactorily and the Burgdorf–Thun Railway entered into a grouping of railway companies that included the Emmental Railway, the Solothurn-Münster Railway, Vereinigte Hutwiler Bahnen, and finally the Oensingen–Balsthal–Bahn. The group, managed by the Emmental–Burgdorf–Thun line (EBT), is 167.2-km-long. Table 4 gives details of the newer motor coaches; there are also 5B- and C-shunting locomotives.

Table 4
BURGDORF–THUN RAILWAY

	Locomotive	Locomotive	Motor Coach	Motor Coach	Motor Coach
Type	Be 4/4	Re 4/4	BDe 2/4	BDe 4/4 I	BDe 4/4 II
Wheel arrangement	Bo-Bo	Bo-Bo	Bo-2	Bo-Bo	Bo-Bo
Length (mm)	12,400	15,410	17,500	22,700	23,700
Wheel base (mm)	8,900	10,700	13,700	18,700	19,500
Wheel diameter (mm)	1,060	1,260	1,060/ 1,040	940	1,040
Total weight (t)	64.7	80	59	60	73
1-hour output (hp)	1,600	6,320	800	1,200	2,860
Maximum speed (km/h)	80	120	80	90	110
Number	10	2	12	8	3
Year built	1932/53	1970	1932/33	1947	1966

Later motor coach for the
Emmental–Burgdorf–Thun
Railway.

The Hanging Railway in the Wupper Valley, West Germany

Wuppertal was created in the 1930s out of three towns, Elberfeld, Barmen and Vohwinkel. The town covers an important industrial district, is densely populated, and has a very extensive transport system comprising railways, trolleys, buses, and, of course, the famous "hanging railway." This line lies mainly above the Wupper river and was built because the narrow valley did not provide enough space for a normal metropolitan railway. For 3 kilometers, the 14-kilometer railway lies above the main road. The railway has been highly successful, serving a town of more than two million inhabitants, but has remained unique, since heavy steel girders hardly beautify such a district.

Built by the firm of Van der Zypen and Charlier in Cologne after the plans of designer E. Langen, the line was completed in five years from 1898 to 1903. Maximum gradients are 27‰, and in the shunting rails of the curves, 45‰. The line lies 8–12 m above the water level of the river and has 20 stations. Girders have a triangular design.

The original vehicles, which had two classes and carried 50 passengers, weighed 16 tons, and were of two types, built in 1900 and 1903. The coaches hang on two bogies, 8 m distant; they can run singly or with one to three trailers. Each of the two bogies has a driving and a running axle (900 mm diameter) with a bogie wheelbase of 1,100 mm.

The 1,900 vehicles have unsprung bogie frames, motors, and supports. In the 1903 vehicles, attempts were made to reduce the unsprung weight and the 36-hp motor was hung under the bogie frame, driving the axle by double gears and a vertical shaft. Consequently, half the train weight is used for traction purposes. Current of 550-v D.C. is supplied through a side conductor rail and sprung current collectors. The main controller has 14 driving and 7 braking positions.

The bogie frames surround the girder and running rails with a very small tolerance (7 mm) so that a derailment is impossible, because even in the case of a fractured axle or wheel the coaches remain suspended. In fact, the safety record of the line is remarkable: in more than 70 years of continuous service there has been only one accident. Side bearers limit any pendulum movement of the coaches.

Great care was taken to make the vehicles run easily in curves, which they enter under the influence of centrifugal forces as smoothly as possible. Speeds were first 30 and later 40 km/h, with a maximum of 55 km/h. The vehicles have three braking systems: Westinghouse airbrake, handbrakes (acting on the running wheels), and an electrical brake.

In 1930, two additional vehicles were delivered, and in 1950, 20 units in an all-steel design arrived.

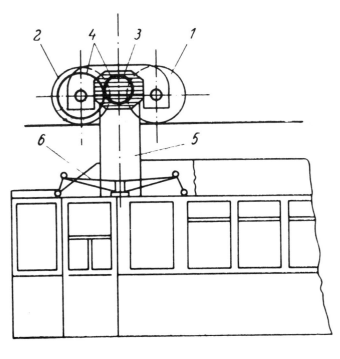

Schematic layout of bogie, drive, and coach support used on Wuppertal "hanging railway" design of 1900.

1. Running Wheel
2. Driving Wheel
3. Motor
4. Guiding Wheel
5. Support Hanger
6. Spring Support

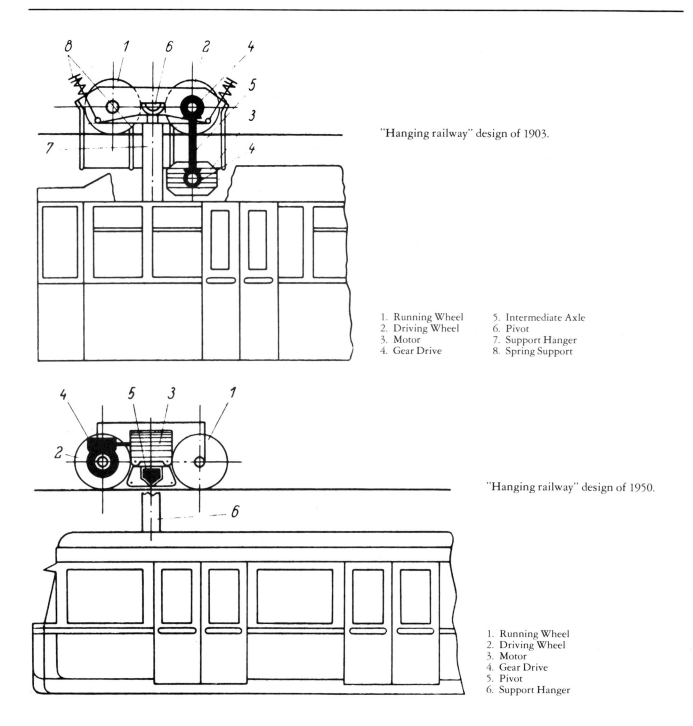

"Hanging railway" design of 1903.

1. Running Wheel	5. Intermediate Axle
2. Driving Wheel	6. Pivot
3. Motor	7. Support Hanger
4. Gear Drive	8. Spring Support

"Hanging railway" design of 1950.

1. Running Wheel
2. Driving Wheel
3. Motor
4. Gear Drive
5. Pivot
6. Support Hanger

In 1941, two of the 1900-series coaches were equipped with new bogies and new electrical equipment. The 1950 vehicles have a tare weight of 11 tons and can take 80 passengers. They have three doors, and the bogie wheel base is 1,500 mm. To reduce noise, special noise-suppressing units were used. The carrying girder is again positioned unsprung in the bogie frames above the bogie pivot, quite close to the running rail. The motors are similar to ordinary nose-suspended ones, partly sprung. The new vehicles also comprise all the modern ideas of coachbuilding, such as improved ventilation, automatic door control, automatic coupling, and so forth. Current has been increased to 600-v.

The "Hanging Railway" of Wuppertal, West Germany.

The New York, New Haven and Hartford Railroad, U.S.A.

In 1900, this railway company electrified 30 kilometers of its Highland division, using 600-v D.C. and third rail. It ordered 37 motor coaches, each with 2 x 50-hp or 2 x 36-hp motors. Their rpm was 853/936 and they weighed 1,120/1,350 kg. The electrical installations were supplied by General Electric and in 1908 the same company provided 11 motor coaches for a further extension of the electric services (12 kilometers); this time 11,000-v 1-phase A.C. was used, having 25 Hz frequency and overhead catenary. Two of the motor coaches had four axles and four 125-hp motors, weighing 60 tons, while nine had two 125-hp motors and weighed 30 tons. In addition, the important four-rail section to Stamford, Connecticut, (35 kilometers) also was electrified with 11,000-v 1-phase A.C. and overhead supply. This last section used locomotive-hauled trains only.

The Zossen–Marienfelde Experiments, Germany

In 1901, experiments were started in Germany with 10,000–12,000-v 3-phase A.C. that were conducted by the so-called Study Group for Electric Express Railways. This group used a 22.5-km-long military railway, Zossen to Marienfelde, near Berlin, for its tests. The highly successful experiments aroused world-wide interest and showed even at that time what efforts an electric railway system could produce. The study group was formed by the two leading German electrical firms: Siemens and Halske and AEG. Both firms built a motor coach and also a locomotive. The test vehicles, designed by Dr. W. Reichel, had to fulfill the following conditions:

1. About 50 seats.
2. Mainline type of service.
3. Maximum speeds of 200 to 250 km/h.
4. Sixteen-ton maximum axle load.
5. Two 3-axle bogies with the middle axle carrying weight only and both outer axles motorized.
6. Four motors producing between 250 and 750 hp.
7. Necessary train and auxiliary brake systems.
8. Current collection from a catenary erected at one side of the railway line.
9. Current tension to be 10–12,000-v, to be reduced on the motor coach to a suitable voltage.

The Siemens and Halske vehicle had a 22,000-mm-long body and a bogie center distance of 14,300 mm, whereby the bogie wheel base was 1,900 mm and the wheel diameter was 1,250 mm. Weights were as follows: electrical part, 42.5 tons; mechanical part, 48 tons; and load, 4 tons, giving a total weight of 94.5 tons. The two front ends of the motor coach were made in a reducing section to lessen wind resistance—an early idea of "streamlining." Windows were fixed and ventilation was carried out through the lantern roof. The coach body sat rigidly on the bogie with its pivot, but the springing was carried out between the bogie frame and axles by leaf and coil springs.

Security of operation was considered an essential part of the design, since experience with such high voltages and speeds was completely lacking. All high-tension parts were so laid out that neither crew nor passengers could get into contact with any part under tension: they were positioned under the vehicle or in the hollow roof space. All switch-gear was air-operated to avoid bringing high-tension cables to the driver's cab. The two pantographs had a vertical mast that carried three sliding contacts pressing spring-loaded against the catenary.

The entire electrical system was divided into two parts so that failure of any one part of the equipment could not prevent the other half from con-

Express motor coach for Zossen–Marienfelde experiments, 1903. Three-phase A.C. 10,000-v.; maximum speed 210 km/h. Design by AEG.

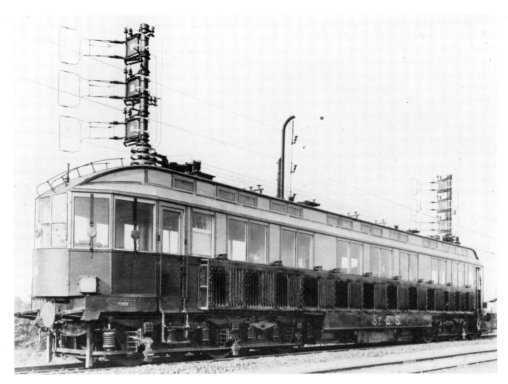

Express motor coach for
Zossen–Marienfelde. Design by
Siemens.

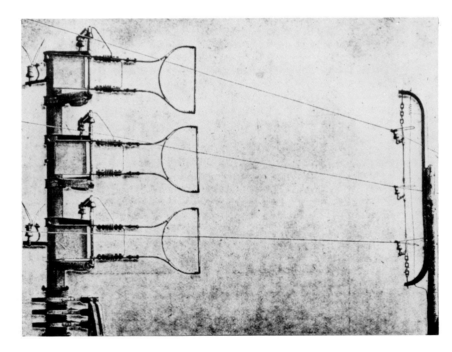

Triple pantograph of express motor coach for
Zossen–Marienfelde.

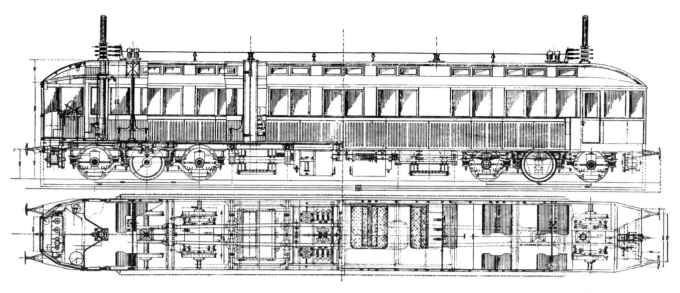

Schematic layout of Siemens test vehicle.

Driver's cab for Siemens test vehicle.

High-tension switch for Siemens test vehicle.

Winter vehicle of the Brighton Coast Railway
by Magnus Volk (England), 1883.

Motor coach of the Snaefell Mountain Railways, Isle of Man, built by
Mather & Platt of Manchester.

Standing cable railways of Lugano. Motor coach ABDe 4/4 4
and 5 for Lugano–Ponte Tresa, built 1952–58.

Standing cable railways of Lugano, leading
to the upper part of the town and the
scenic hills of San Salvatore and Monte Bré.

Standing cable railways of Lugano, leading to the upper part of the town and the scenic hills of San Salvatore and Monte Bré.

The "Hanging Railway" of Wuppertal, West Germany.

Rack locomotive and adhesion motor coach for Stansstad–Engelberg Railway.

Train for the Vienna–Baden Express Railway, Austria.

1896 adhesion motor coach for Stansstad–Engelberg Railway.

tinuing to function. The two transformers also were mounted under the frame and supplied the two motors of each bogie with 1,150–1,850-v current. Variation in current was achieved through star-delta connection as well as through resistances. Each transformer weighed 6,150 kg and the two motors weighed 8,150 kg.

Motors were axle-mounted without gear transmission and had a maximum rpm of 900. The 28 resistances were positioned at the side and operated by a rack-wheel. The driver's cab contained the necessary speedometer, voltmeter, current indicator, and so on.

The other motor coach was supplied by AEG and had level front faces. The main differences from the Seimens and Halske design were as follows: the motors were not positioned on the axles but were placed on hollow shafts surrounding the axles and were vertically sprung. Power transmission was carried out by leaf springs from the hollow shafts to the wheels. This design allowed for smaller but more complex motors. The starter was of the liquid type with a soda solution as coolant and a copper tube cooler. This liquid starter permitted an even insertion and cutting-out of resistances. Control of the vehicle was carried out from the driver's cab by mechanical devices that operated the contactor gear mounted under the floor.

The experiments showed clearly that electric traction was capable of achieving 200 km/h in safety; obviously, the experiments were far ahead of their time and it took 50 to 60 years until the lessons learned from these tests were put to practical use.

The Fribourg–Murten–Ins Railway, Switzerland

The Fribourg–Murten section of this mainline was opened in 1898 and electrified in 1903, together with the extension to Ins. The line is 32.3-km-long and belongs today to the GFM group. Originally, 750-v D.C. was used with third rail in open country and catenary in stations.

Bo-Bo motor coach with four 60-hp motors, 1,200-v D.C., for Biel–Teufelen–Ins Railway (Switzerland).

Bo'-2' motor coach of 1931 (1946) for the GFM group of railways; 48.8-ton weight, 90 km/h maximum speed.

Bo'-Bo' motor coach of 1966, 64-ton weight, 1,460 hp/1-hour and 100 km/h maximum speed, for GFM group of railways.

This was the first steam railway in Switzerland to be changed over to electric traction. The railway ordered four 4-axle motor coaches, each with four 100-hp motors, supplied by MFO. The vehicles weighed 33 tons, the electrical system accounting for 12 tons. Total length was 17,300/19,800 mm; bogie wheel base, 2,600 mm; total wheel base, 14,000/14,100 mm; wheel diameter, 1,010 mm; and gear ratio, 1:4. The vehicles carried 48 to 56 passengers and had a maximum speed of 55 km/h. In 1931, a fifth, more powerful motor coach was added, but in 1946 the line was changed to 15,000-v A.C. 1-phase, 16⅔ Hz; seven motor coaches were ordered. The

above-mentioned fifth vehicle was reconstructed for the new current system.

The Electric Railway Trieste–Opcina, Italy

In 1902, the meter-gauge line from Trieste to Opcina was opened. The railway was built in three sections: in the first, the motor coach ran on an adhesion section, on the second, it was pushed uphill by a rack locomotive (using Strub rackrail system), and on the third, adhesion operation was used again. Current was 600-v D.C. and the vehicle had bow collectors. Electrical installation was supplied by AEG-Vienna.

The Pyrénéan Railway: Villefranche–Vernet– Les Bains–La Tour de Carol and branch to Bourg–Madame–La Tour de Carol, France

The Midi railway had received a license in 1880 to build this line, but it was not until 1911 that the first section was completed and 1928 when the second one followed. The lines, electrified in 1932, lead through very wild and mountainous country, reaching their highest point in La Tour de Carol on the Spanish-French frontier at 1,230 m above sea level.

This meter-gauge railway has no less than 390 curves, gradients reach 60‰, and the difference in heights to be overcome is 805 m. There are 17 tunnels with a total length of 2,769 m. Well known is the "hanging bridge" over the Tet river with a height of 80 m. The railway uses 800-v D.C. with third rail supply of current. Passenger as well as freight cars are hauled. All vehicles are 4-axled with two bogies, have an output of 300 hp, and weigh 28–32 tons. They reach speeds of 55 km/h and are equipped with Sprague-Westinghouse multiple-unit control.

A similar line (formerly belonging to the PLM railway) is the meter-gauge line from Le Fayet to Chamonix, which is equipped with comparable vehicles. This line was opened in 1901 and has gradients up to 90‰.

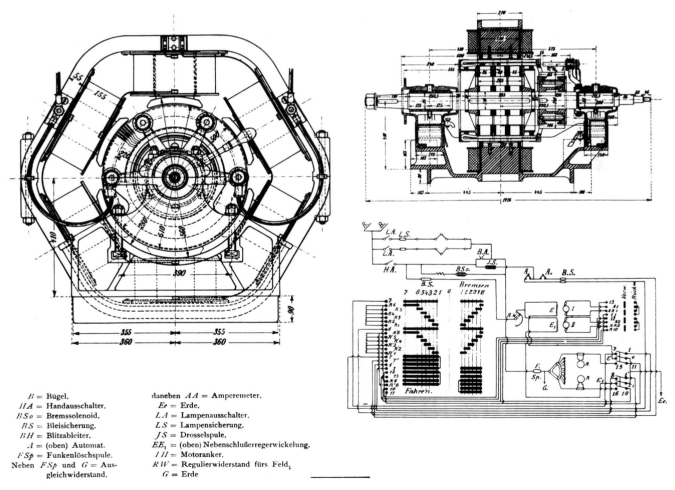

B = Bügel.	daneben AA = Amperemeter.
HA = Handausschalter.	Ee = Erde.
BSo = Bremssolenoid.	LA = Lampenausschalter.
BS = Bleisicherung.	LS = Lampensicherung.
BH = Blitzableiter.	JS = Drosselspule.
A = (oben) Automat.	EE_1 = (oben) Nebenschlußerregerwickelung.
FSp = Funkenlöschspule.	$I II$ = Motoranker.
Neben FSp und G = Aus-	RW = Regulierwiderstand fürs Feld,
gleichwiderstand.	G = Erde.

Layout and diagram of 100-hp, 700 rpm 600-v D.C. motor built by AEG for Trieste–Opcina Railway (Italy).

1902 freight motor coach for P.L.M.
Line St. Gervais-le-Fayet–
Chamonix.

Freight motor coach of the Pyrenean Railroad (Villefranche–La Tour de Carol).

The Electric Railway Tabor–Bechyn, Czechoslovakia

In 1903, the standard-gauge railway from Tabor to Bechyn, 24-km-long and with 35‰ gradients, was electrified. The work was carried out by one of the pioneering firms of electric traction, Krizik of Prague. The electrification is historically important since a three-wire system was used, two wires with 2 x 700-v D.C. supply. Each motor coach had two bow collectors that took the current to the 4 D.C. series-connected motors.

The motor coaches were 4-axled, output was originally 30 hp (1 hour) per motor, and gear ratio was 1:5. Speed was regulated by two series-parallel contactors. Other particulars were motor weight,

935 kg; 40-passenger capacity; speed on level sections, 30 km/h, and on gradient, 15 km/h; total length, 15,000 mm; bogie wheel base, 2,000 mm; distance between bogie centers, 9,000 mm; wheel diameter, 850/900 mm; weight, 18.8 tons; and electrical system weight, 5.3 tons.

The railway ran successfully for 35 years when it was rebuilt with 1,500-v D.C. The motor coaches also were rebuilt, two in 1931 and one in 1938. One was destroyed by fire. Although the coach bodies were retained, the electrical installations were totally renewed. After rebuilding, the vehicles weighed 25 tons and the four new motors had 55 kw output at 750 rpm and 27 km/h. The rebuilding, completed in 1938, was carried out by Skoda of Prague and the original supplier, Krizik. Some of the early technical components were presented to the Technical Museum in Prague.

Opened in 1904, the line is 18.2-km-long, and, because this was a long line for the period, it was undesirable to use D.C. The motor coaches therefore were equipped with Winter–Eichberg A.C. motors. Originally, it was a 2-phase line with a single overhead wire and a frequency of 42 Hz. Tension was 2,400-v and later 3,000-v and 50 Hz. The railway has meter-gauge and leads through a wild Alpine valley with many viaducts, bridges, tunnels, and gradients up to 46‰. The line first rises 390 m and then descends 66 m.

Today, the railway is in full use and all installations function well after over 70 years' work. Original motor coaches had two 2-axle bogies with two 40-hp motors. Other particulars were: 800 rpm; 1:5.07 gear ratio; 800-mm wheel diameter; motor weight, 1,385 kg; 40 sitting and 20 standing passenger capacity; weight, 19.6 tons; length, 11,000 mm.

The Stubai Valley Railway in Austria

This railway connects the capital of the Tyrol in Austria, Innsbruck, with an important tourist center, the beautiful Stubai Valley (Fulpmes). The line also is historically important as the first high-tension 1-phase A.C. line in Europe.

The Montreux–Bernese–Oberland Railways, Switzerland

This important narrow-gauge network was built and electrified between 1901 and 1904, having 63 kilometers meter-gauge length with maximum gradi-

Motor coach and trailer for the Stubaital Railway of Austria.

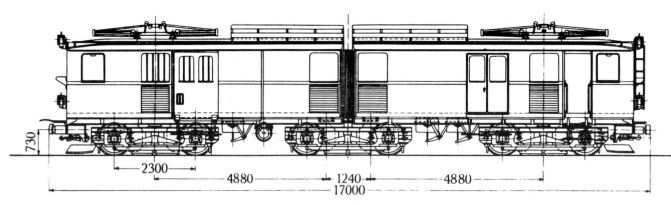

Schematic layout of 6-axle Bo'-Bo'-Bo' luggage motor van of Montreux–Bernese–Oberland Railway (MOB). Supplied in 1932 by Brown, Boveri, & CIE.

Four-axle lightweight motorcoach train of 1944–45 for MOB luggage motor van.

ents of 72‰. Working conditions are very severe—the line from Montreux rises 720 m in 14.2 kilometers and extends to heights above sea level of 1,150 and 1,280 m. The total differences in height that have to be overcome on the journey from Montreux to Zweisimmen are 1,936 m.

The railway first used 750-v D.C. and later 900-v. In the beginning, six 4-axled motor coaches were ordered for Montreux–Les Avants with four 30–65-hp motors. Weights were 22–28 tons. Speeds varied according to gradients between 15 and 40 km/h. Trains of two motor coaches weighed 48 to 90 tons, each motor coach being driven as a separate unit. During the line's existence, several vehicles were acquired and are described in Table 5.

One of the most interesting designs is the 6-axle "luggage motor van." Its output is 1,000 hp/1-hour at 21.8 km and 11,800 kg tractive effort. Maximum

Table 5
MONTREUX–BERNESE–OBERLAND RAILWAYS

No.	Type	Motors	Year	Weight in Tons
1	4-axle m/coach	4 x 30 hp = 120 hp	1901	22
3	4-axle m/coach	4 x 45 hp = 180 hp	1903	27
17	4-axle m/coach	4 x 65 hp = 260 hp	1904/8	28
4	4-axle m/coach	4 x 120 hp = 480 hp	1912	33.5
2	4-axle m/coach	4 x 165 hp = 660 hp	1924	36
2	6-axle m/coach	6 x 200 hp = 1,200 hp	1932	63
6	4-axle m/coach	4 x 150 hp = 600 hp	1944/5	35.7

tractive effort is 18,000 kg and top speed is 60 km/h. The low axle-load of 11 tons and the weight in working order of 62.85 tons required a 6-axle fully motorized vehicle; it has the wheel arrangement Bo-Bo-Bo.

Other main details are as follows: length, 17,000 mm; bogie wheel base, 2,300 mm; total wheel base, 11,000 mm; and wheel diameter, 945 mm. The coach body consists of two close-coupled parts, connected by a concertina-link. This design was required because of the many and narrow curves (down to 35 m radius) the vehicles traverse; each vehicle half rests on the bogies in 3-point suspension.

There are two drivers' cabs and a luggage compartment, as well as two engine rooms and a wash room. The six 8-pole motors are nose-suspended and have a 1-hour output of 167 hp or short-time of 200 hp. Recuperative brake systems are available, as well as magnetic rail brakes. The vehicles have two pantographs, main switch, and an electropneumatic camshaft control with 18 pneumatic steps. Suppliers were BBC and Neuhausen.

Lightweight motor coaches arrived in 1944–45 that clearly show the substantial progress made in 15 years on the design of modern electric vehicles. The new motor coaches, supplied by BBC/Schlieren,

Six-axle Bo-Bo-Bo luggage motor van of the Montreux–Bernese–Oberland Railway (MBO).

have the following main dimensions: weight, 36 tons; electrical part, 11 tons; approximate total weight of a train (two motor coaches and two trailers), 80 tons; 1-hour output, 440 kw at 37.2 km/h; gear ratio, 1:5.67; wheel diameter, 850 mm; and maximum speed, 75 km/h. The newer vehicles have three brake systems—recuperative, resistance, and rail brake—which can be run in multiple-unit control with a step-controller with 22 running and 31 braking steps. The power-transmission used is the BBC springpot drive. In 1968, four more twin-motor coaches, series ABDe 8/8, were ordered, with an hourly output of 8 x 150 hp = 1200 hp and a maximum speed of 70 km/h.

The Mersey and Wirral Lines, England

This was the first steam railway to be electrified in England. It opened in 1886 to connect the Wirral peninsula with Liverpool and to link Birkenhead and its surroundings with a tunnel under the Mersey River. The reason for this early electrification was that two-thirds of the line were in tunnel, and steam traction with its smoke nuisance had reached the limit of its capacity. The electrification includes 11.7 kilometers of line with a rail length of 20 kilometers. The line was converted in 1903 with Metropolitan-Vickers supplying total installation and all vehicles. The line had two conductor-rails (positive and negative) and used 650-v D.C.

In the beginning, 26 motor coaches and 33 trailers were ordered; they were to form two-, three-,

and five-coach trains, giving three-minute service between Liverpool central and Birkenhead (Hamilton Square). The motor coaches had four nose-suspended motors (two per bogie) with a 1-hour rating of 100 hp. The same firm in 1923 supplied two more motor coaches and four trailers, and in 1924 it furnished a five-coach train with 125-hp motors.

After some time it was obvious that the Mersey Line, which only led to Birkenhead, could not cope with the ever-increasing traffic developing around the River Dee, West Kirby, and New Brighton. It was decided to electrify these lines as well. New three-coach trains were built both by the workshops and by Metropolitan-Cammell; the electrical parts were supplied by BTH. The trains run as three- or six-coach trains and are equipped with multiple-unit control. Each train consists of motor coach, trailer, and driving trailer, the units being close-coupled. The three-unit train has 181 seats and substantial standing room. Each motor coach has four 135-hp (1-hour) or 93-hp (continuous) output.

The Liverpool–Southport and Crossens and Ormskirk Lines of the LMS Railway (later Midland Section of BR), England

In 1904, the former Lancashire and Yorkshire Railway electrified its 30-km-long line between Liverpool and Southport and in 1913 extended this suburban network to Ormskirk and Crossens, whereby 60 kilometers of line with 150 kilometers of rail

1938 motorcoach train for the Wirral and Merseyside electrifications—Liverpool.

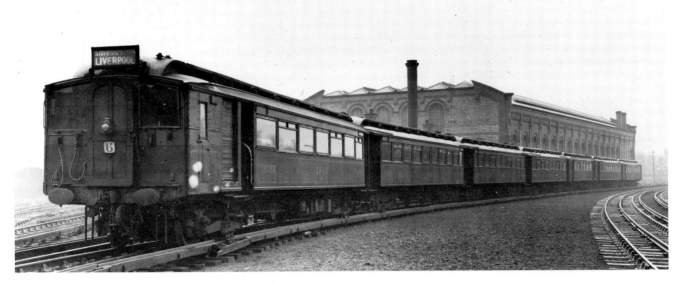

Motorcoach train of 1924 for the Liverpool–Southport electrification of the Lancashire and Yorkshire Railway.

600-v three-coach train in multiple-unit service on the Liverpool–Southport Line. Supplied in 1939 by the English Electric Co.

length were finally electrified. These lines always had substantial suburban traffic, which increased with electrification.

Vehicles for the 1904 and 1910 work were supplied by Dick, Kerr & Company (later English Electric). The line used 3- and 4-current rail and 650-v D.C. Trains were made up of three, four, five,

and six units. Each motor coach had four 150-hp motors and weighed 44.7 tons, and each trailer was 26.9 tons.

In 1926, Metropolitan-Vickers supplied the electrical parts for 11 motor coaches. These had four 265-hp motors.

In 1939, English Electric supplied 59 motor

coaches and 59 trailers, as well as 34 driving trailers. The new vehicles were designed and built in the railway workshops in Derby. They were constructed according to state-of-the-art ideas as self-supporting frameless units: frame, walls, and roof formed a tubular unit that transmitted all forces. The saving in weight was substantial, a three-coach train weighing only 90.5 tons, whereby the motor coach weighed 40.75 tons and the trailer, 23.5 tons. Each motor coach had four nose-suspended 235-hp/1-hour motors and 184-hp continuous output. Wheel diameter was 914 mm and gear ratio, 64:17. Total length of a three-coach train was 63,700 mm; it had a capacity of 268 seats and 352 standing; maximum speed was 96 km/h.

The Lancaster–Heysham–Morecambe Electrification of the Midland Railway, England

The Midland Railway electrified its important suburban sections between Lancaster, Heysham, and Morecambe in 1908. The line was 15-km-long with a 34-kilometer rail length, and used single-phase A.C. of 6,600-v and 25 Hz. Electrification caused considerable difficulties and costs because of the narrow profile of this line. Originally, there were three trains, each with a motor coach and a trailer. Siemens Brothers supplied two of the electrical outfits and British Westinghouse (later Metropolitan-Vickers) manufactured the third. The Siemens control system was electrical and Westinghouse's was electropneumatic.

Motor coaches were 20,130 mm long and accommodated 72 seated passengers, with room for 58 and 36 standing passengers. Trailers were 13,115 mm long and had a driver's cab; they had 54 seats. Bogie wheel base was 2,470 mm for the driving bogie and 2,440 mm for the running bogie. Wheel diameter was 1,100 mm. Each motor coach was able to haul two 26-ton passenger coaches and provided a 15–20-minute timetable. The two motors per coach had an output of 180 hp (Siemens) and 150 hp (Westinghouse). The Siemens vehicle had bow collectors and the Westinghouse employed pantographs.

Lancaster–Heysham–Morecambe electrification; motor coaches by Metropolitan-Vickers.

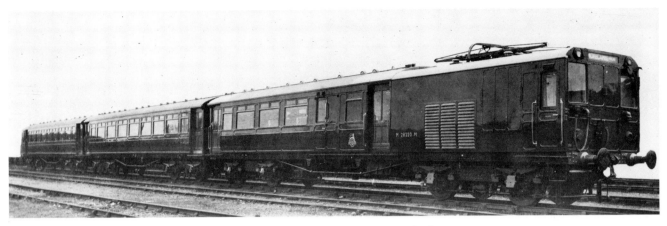

Experimental 6,600-v, 1-phase A.C. 25 Hz train for Lancaster–Heysham–Morecambe line.

Motor coach of the Long Island Railroad.

The Long Island Railroad, U.S.A.

In 1905, this line electrified 60 kilometers of a 160-kilometer rail length with 650-v D.C. and third rail. The line was a subsidiary of the Pennsylvania Railroad and was the first U.S. mainline to run full-scale electric service. Westinghouse supplied the electrical installations.

There were 135 motor coaches with 2 x 2-axle bogies; one of the bogies was motorized with 2 x 200-hp motors. Dimensions include gear ratio, 25:58; motor weight, 2,980 kg; 573 rpm; 914-mm wheel diameter; tare weight, 37.2 tons; 52 seats. The railroad intended to run three seven-coach trains with two five-motor coaches, the latter with electropneumatic control gear by Westinghouse. Maximum speed was 92 km/h. Later, 225 additional motor coaches were ordered, each weighing 52 tons with two 210-hp motors per vehicle.

The Murnau–Oberammergau Railway of the Bavarian Local Railways (later DR and DB), Germany

This line is 23-km-long, has standard gauge, and has gradients up to 30‰. Siemens supplied the installations for the 1905 electrification of the line, which uses 1-phase A.C. of 5,500-v and 16 Hz. Traffic

Motor coach and trailer for the Murnau–Oberammergau line of the Bavarian Local Railway Co. with 2 x 100-hp Siemens 1-phase A.C. motors.

started with 3-axle motor coaches, which originally had two 100-hp compensated series motors with a transmission gear ratio of 1:5 and 800-mm wheel diameter. An oil-cooled transformer was located under the frame. Trains, consisting of summer and winter coaches, had speeds of 40 km/h on level surfaces and 14 to 17 km/h on gradients, with a maximum speed of 60 km/h. Other main data were: total weight, 30 tons; electrical part, 11.7 tons; total length, 13,500 mm.

The Martigny–Chatelard Railway and its Motor Coaches, France

This meter-gauge line was opened in 1906 and has three sections: the 4.8-kilometer adhesion line in the Rhone Valley between Martigny and Vernayaz, the 2.5-kilometer rack section as far as Salvan, and the 12-kilometer adhesion section to the French frontier where the Chamonix Line is reached. The line has many tunnels and viaducts and has gradients up to 200‰ on rack and 70‰ on the adhesion sections.

A Strub rack system is used. This railway climbs between Martigny (470 m above sea level), Salvan (1,937 m), and the frontier at Finhaut (1,227 m)— a difference in heights of 757 m. The railway used 750-v D.C. and later 800-v D.C., which is supplied to the vehicles by catenary on the Vernayaz–Martigny section and by third conductor rail on the rest of the system. Electrical installations were supplied by a forerunner of Sécherôn and MFO, and mechanical parts were supplied by SLM and Schlieren.

Vehicles consisted of 300-hp rack locomotives and 260- and 150-hp rack-and-adhesion motor coaches. Two rack locomotives that were used as freight locomotives were sold to the Villars–Chesières–Bretaye Line. The motor coaches have two 2-axle bogies with 10,500 mm distance of pivots.

Bogies contained a rack axle and adhesion driving axle, each with its own motor, whereby both axles had the same circumferential speed. The drive contained sprung gearwheels and a universal coupling. There was a special controller to supervise the changeover from catenary to current rail. Motor coaches also were supplied to run with trailers, whereby a kind of multiple-unit control was used.

Martigny–Châtelard Railway. Vehicles for third rail.

Martigny–Châtelard Railway. Sécherôn motor coach of 1906.

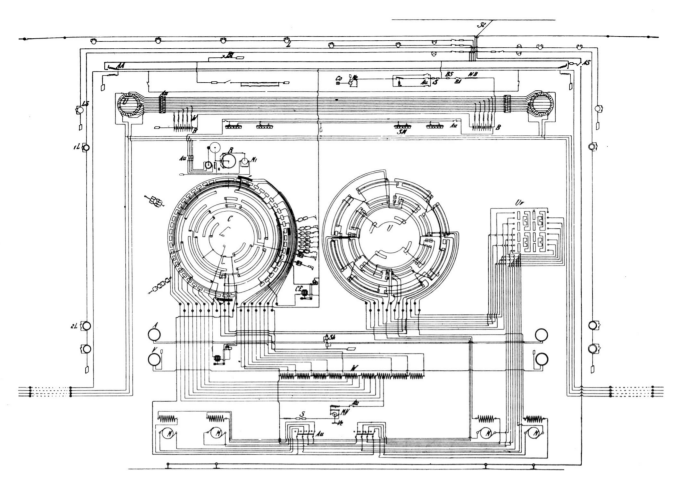

M = Motor	AA = Automatic cutoff	BS = Battery safety
C = Control	B1 = Lightning rod	Co = Compressor
U = Reverse	St = Current receiver for driving cable control	M2 = 3 horsepower motor
Uv = Reverse drive	AS = Current reverse for 3rd rail or air control	Ve = Ventilator
W = Resistance	V = Voltage meter	MV = Ventilator motor
GE = Spark extinguisher	R = Starter control apparatus	L = Lamp
A = Ampere meter	M1 = 1/20 horsepower motor	LS = Signal lamp
Sh = Ampere meter shunt or cutoff	B = Battery	1L = 1 Signal lamp
Au = Cutoff	WB = Battery resistance	2L = 2 Signal lamp
S = Safety	BA = Battery cutout	

Martigny–Châtelard Railway. Diagram of electrical installations of 4 x 60-240 hp motor coach of 1906.

In 1957–61, SAAS and Schindler supplied five motorcoach trains consisting of motor coach ABFeh 4/4 and driving trailer ABFt 4. These trains have a capacity of 210 passengers and weigh 64 tons; there is also a mail and luggage compartment. The trains can be controlled remotely by an electromagnetic contactor gear.

Other particulars are: length, 18,000 mm; bogie pivot distance, 11,500 mm; bogie wheel base, 2,970 mm; driving wheel diameter, 860 mm; gear transmission ratios, adhesion/rack, 1:10.52/1:7.48. Total weight is 34.5 tons, with the electrical part weighing 8.6 tons. One-hour output is 760 hp at 17.7 kilometers.

In 1933, an agreement between this railway company and the French PLM Line provided that they would also service the French Vallorcine–Mortroc–Le Planet Line.

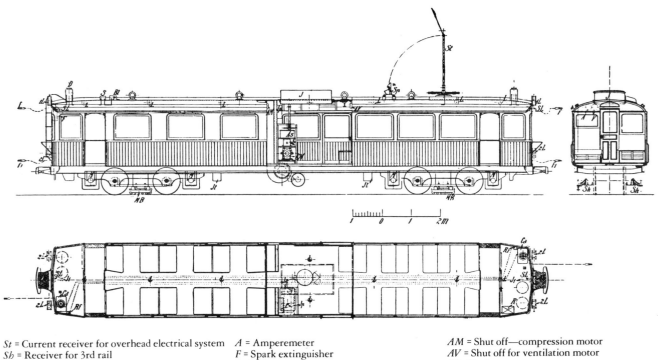

St = Current receiver for overhead electrical system
Sh = Receiver for 3rd rail
Sp = Safety catch for receiver
Bl = Lightning rod
D = Automatic shutoff
L = Lamp
1L = 1 Lamp
2L = 2 Lamp
SL = Signal lamp
V = Voltage meter

A = Amperemeter
F = Spark extinguisher
J = Self starter
As = Starter's control apparatus
J2 = Commutator
CM = Compressor motor
C = Compressor
Ca = Operation of the starter control apparatus
MB = Magnetic brake
M = Motor

AM = Shut off—compression motor
AV = Shut off for ventilation motor
Rf = Resistance
Jp = Current reverse receiver, 3rd rail air control
R = Accumulator resistance
J1 = the shut-off operation
f = the engage shut-off for 1 cable (for starter)
f1 = the engage shut-off for 4 cables (for starter)
Jt = Circuit breaker for pivot mounting motors

Martigny–Châtelard Railway. Schematic illustration of 1906 Sécherôn motor coach.

Martigny–Châtelard Railway.
760 hp motor coach, supplied in
1957–63 by Sécherôn.

New York Central and Hudson River Railroad motor coach of 1904.

Bogie for above 1904 motor coach.

The New York Central and Hudson River Railroad, U.S.A.

Between 1904 and 1908, this railway electrified the so-called 54.6-kilometer Hudson Line from New York to Croton, and also the 38.7-kilometer Harlem Line from New York to White Plains, with 660-v D.C. Third rail locomotives were ordered for this intensive service as well as 137 all-steel motor coaches. These had two 2-axle bogies, one of which was fully motorized with two 200-hp motors.

Other main dimensions were: driving wheel diameter, 914 mm; running wheel diameter, 838 mm; gear ratio, 1:1.88; and tare weight, 46.5 tons. In addition, 63 trailers and five freight cars were ordered. All vehicles had Sprague multiple-unit con-trol furnished by General Electric, which also supplied all electrical installations. Maximum speed was 85 km/h. Each train consisted of five motor coaches and three trailers.

The Electrification of the Camden–Atlantic City, N.J. Line, U.S.A.

The above line belonged to the West Jersey and Sea-Shore Railroad when it was electrified in 1906 with 650-v D.C. Catenary and third rail was used. The electrification comprised a 104-kilometer main line and 16 kilometers of branch lines. General Electric supplied 93 motor coaches and later 15 all-steel

Motor coach and trailer for the
Stubaital Railway of Austria.

Six-axle Bo'-Bo'-Bo' luggage motor van of
the Montreux–Bernese–Oberland Railway
(MBO).

Rhaetian Railroad motor coach.

Cologne–Bonn Railway. Motorcoach
trains of 1950–56.

"Blue Trains" for suburban sections, Glasgow, B.R.

"Variable-Inclination" motorcoach train of the F.S.

Lightweight motorcoach train, series Yoa2, for Sweden.

"Variable-Inclination" motor coach
driver's cab with control desk.

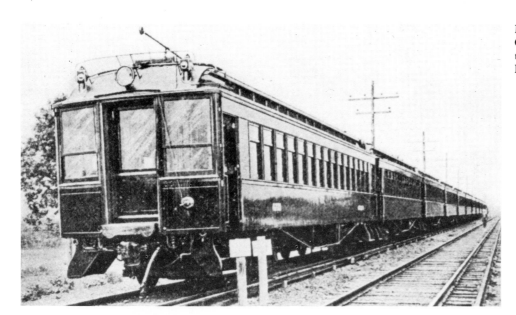

Motorcoach train for the Camden–Atlantic City Line of the West Jersey and Seashore Railroad of 1906.

Monthey–Champéry Railway (Switzerland) 4-axle motor coach for rack and adhesion service, built in 1908.

motor coaches (52 tons in weight). All had two 2-axle bogies, one of which was motorized with two 240-hp motors.

Pertinent data includes: gear ratio, 29:46; wheel diameter, 914 mm; motor weight, 2,820 kg; 456 rpm; tare weight, 48 tons; there were 56 seats and a luggage and mail compartment. Trains consisted of five to six coaches without trailers, all run with Sprague multiple-unit control. Maximum speed was 105 km/h.

The Monthey–Champéry Railway, Switzerland

Opened in 1906, this line is 11.4-km-long and has meter-gauge and maximum gradients of 136‰. It reaches 640 m above sea level and uses Strub rack-rail. For its mixed rack-and-adhesion services, it uses motor coaches that also cover the maximum adhesion gradient of 50‰.

Motor coaches have two 2-axle bogies that are fully motorized with one axle carrying the adhesion

Aigle–Ollon–Monthey–Champéry Line, 4-axle motor coach of 1951.

motor and the other carrying the rack motor. The adhesion axles are coupled together by rods, while the rack drive consists of one driven and one carrying axle. The vehicles have two bow collectors. Other data of interest: distance of bogie centers, 7,500 mm; bogie wheel base, 1,800 mm; maximum tractive effort, 8,000 kg; speeds were 25/10 km/h on adhesion/rack sections.

The Cologne–Bonn Railway and its Vehicles, Germany

Since 1906, a standard-gauge express railway has connected Bonn with its suburbs along the river Rhine. Bonn's stature as capital of Western Germany has considerably increased the importance of this line. The railway is 106-km-long and has two main lines: one along the river via Wesselring called the Rhein–Uferbahn, and the other running through the hill district via Bruehl, called the Vorgebirgsbahn. In addition to passenger traffic, the line provides extensive freight service—in 1955, 16 million passengers and 11 million tons of freight were moved.

Of its 258-kilometer rail length, 116 kilometers are electrified, all with catenary and 1,200-v D.C. In addition to its other vehicles, the railway started with 10 electric motor coaches with 2 x 130-hp motors, supplied by Siemens. The vehicles had two 2-axle bogies, gear ratio was 1:3.1, and rpm was 700. Wheel diameter was 950 mm, motor weight was 2,500 kg, tare weight was 27 tons, and each coach had 57 seats.

Motorcoach trains were ordered from 1936 to 1940, and even more were delivered in 1950, sup-

Original trains of the Cologne–Bonn Railway, 1906.

Modern trains of Cologne–Bonn Railway from 1959.

Cologne–Bonn Railway. Motorcoach trains of 1950–56.

plied by Westwaggon and Siemens. The vehicles are twin-motor coaches of wheel-arrangement Bo-2 + 2-Bo, which together with two driving trailers form a train. The vehicles were designed for 110 km/h; their main dimensions are found in Table 6.

Vehicles are equipped with cam-shaft operated

step-controllers and all have electric resistance brakes; trains up to six vehicles can be run. Motors are nose-suspended and are coupled in series of two's. There are twelve series and nine parallel steps.

In 1959, a lightweight motor coach of wheel-arrangement Bo-Bo was ordered. The vehicle was supplied by Westwagon, Deutz, SSW, and VLMW in a joint effort to produce a vehicle that was economical to run, incorporated the latest ideas of coach building, and satisfied passengers with real traveling comfort by using lightweight materials in the body and bogies. Tare weight consequently was reduced to 30 tons to produce a vehicle that is air-smooth and can run at 130 km/h. The four motors have a 1-hour output of 102 hp. Driving is accomplished again through cam-operated contactor gear with full automation of operation. The bogies are of the Minden-Deutz type with traction rods. Bogie wheel base is 2,200 mm, wheel diameter is 760 mm, and the pivots are only 745 mm above railheads. The bogie with railbrake but without motors weighs 3.57 tons, with motors about 5 tons. Body length is 24,400 mm, distance of bogie centers is 16,300 mm, and there are 72 seats with room for 78 standees during rush-hour traffic. The railway vehicles have been attractively painted and are fully air-conditioned.

Table 6
COLOGNE–BONN RAILWAY

	Twin Motor Coach	Driving Trailer
Weight, tare (tons)	57	20
Seats	112 or 94 + luggage and mail part.	71/73
Total length (mm)	18,500	18,500
Bogie center distance (mm)	12,800	12,800
Bogie wheel base (mm)	2,600	2,600
Wheel diameter (mm)	960	960
1-hour output of 4 motors at 1,050-v	4 x 108 Kw	————

Early Experiments in Sweden

In Sweden, two lines six- and seven-km-long were electrified in 1905, from Tomteboda to Vaertan and from Stockholm to Jaerfva. Many tests were conducted and 1-phase of 5,000–15,000-v was used. Frequencies tested were 15 and 25, and various overhead lines were investigated. In addition to the locomotives ordered, AEG supplied two motor coaches that had 115-hp Winter–Eichberg motors, four poles, and were built for a stator voltage of 6–7,000-v. Gear ratio was 1:4.26 and 1:2.96 and wheel diameter was 1,000 mm.

Traffic on the Stockholm–Jaerfva Line was accomplished by two passenger trains, one consisting of two motor coaches and two trailers, the other driven by a locomotive supplied by British Westinghouse. On the other line, only freight traffic run by a SSW locomotive was initially offered. Other electrical installations were supplied by Asea.

Also in 1907, the 891-meter-gauge Oestgoetlands Central Railway (MOJ) was electrified, for which Asea supplied motor coach No. C6A, later Xalp. The railway used 10,000-v 1-phase A.C. of 25 Hz. The 3-axle vehicle was 8,800 mm long, had two 12-kw motors, and could carry 35 passengers. Later it was rebuilt and appeared in the form shown in the illustration. Wheel base was 4,200 mm and driving wheel diameter, 800 mm. The middle running axle had a diameter of 740 mm.

Early Swedish motor coach.

10,000-v, 1-phase 25 Hz motor coach of 1907 for Oestgoetlands Central Railway of Sweden, supplied by ASEA.

The two Rigi Railways, Switzerland

The Rigi has been one of the famous tourist attractions of Switzerland since the early nineteenth century. The first real mountain railway of Europe was the Vitznau–Rigi Railway, built from 1871 to 1875, which is a memorial to the pioneer of rack railways, Nikolaus Riggenbach. The length of the line via Staffelhoehe to Kulm is 6,858 m, climbing 1,311 m, and having gradients of 60 to 250‰. The railway has standard gauge and in the center uses the well-known ladder-like Riggenbach rack-rail. The railway was electrified in 1937.

After the great success of the Vitznau line, another railway opened at Arth on Zuger Lake linking with the Gotthard Line, which was under construction. The Arth–Rigi–Bahn also has standard gauge and consists of an adhesion and rack section. The first leads from Arth to Goldau, is 2,650 m long, and has gradients of 66‰. The mountain section is 4,204 m long; it too uses the Riggenbach rack system and has gradients up to 200‰. The line was opened in 1875 and electrified in 1907.

Motor coaches for the Vitznau line were ordered in 1937 from SLM-Winterthur, while BBC supplied the electrical installations. The coach body rests on two 2-axle bogies, the mountain-sided one carrying the driving motors and brake system while the valley-sided one is the running bogie only. Construction is of the self-supporting all-steel type. The motors are nose-suspended, the main axle carrying the driving rack wheel, the latter mounted loosely with its transmission gear on a drum that sits freely on the main axle.

Main data of the vehicle and line are as follows: 1,500-v D.C., overhead catenary; two motors; twin-rack transmission gear, 1:21.2; weight in working order (72 passengers), 22 tons. A leading trailer can be pushed uphill. Maximum speed downhill is 12 km/h, and uphill, 18 km/h. One-hour rating is 450 hp at 14.6 km/h and 8,000 kg tractive effort.

Turning again to the Arth–Rigi Line, the first three motor coaches had the following main data: four axles with two motors of 135 hp equalling 270 hp; transmission ratio 1:14.75; speed, 7.3 km/h; running wheel diameter, 968 mm; and rack wheel diameter, 955 mm. The vehicles had wooden bodies. Bogie wheel base is 2,450 mm (2,050 mm). Weight was 23.35 tons, the electrical part being 5.5 tons. In 1911, a 3-axle motor coach with the same output was acquired and, in 1925, a 4-axle vehicle with 2 x 144-hp motors equalling 288-hp/1-hour output was ordered.

In the years 1949 to 1958, SLM and SAAS supplied three push-and-pull trains, consisting of motor coach BDeh 2/4 and driving trailer Bt. The

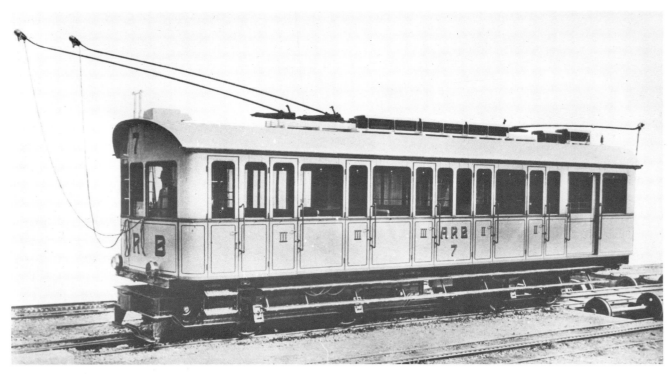

Original motor coach of the Arth–Rigi Line of 1907, built by SLM-Winterthur.

Triebdrehgestell

Bergseite

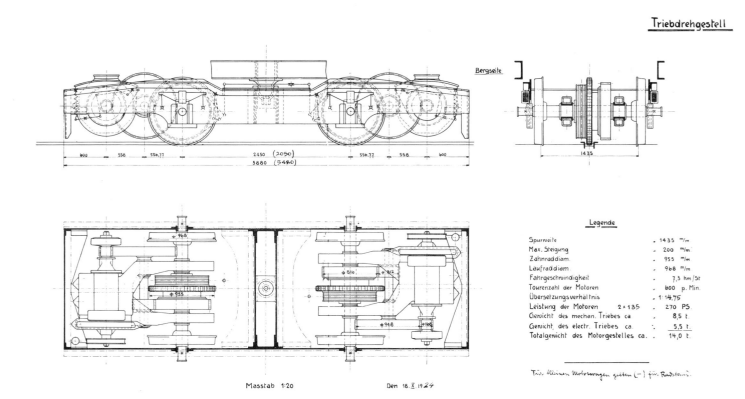

Legende

Spurweite	.	1435 m/m
Max. Steigung	.	200 m/m
Zahnraddiam.	.	955 m/m
Laufraddiam.	.	968 m/m
Fahrgeschwindigkeit	.	7,3 km/St
Tourenzahl der Motoren	.	600 p. Min.
Übersetzungsverhältnis	.	1:14,75
Leistung der Motoren 2 × 135	.	270 PS
Gewicht des mechan. Triebes ca	.	8,5 t.
Gewicht des electr. Triebes ca	.	5,5 t.
Totalgewicht des Motorgestelles ca	.	14,0 t.

Masstab 1:20   Den 18. X. 1924

Layout of bogie for SLM-Winterthur motor coach.

1,500-v D.C. motor coach for SLM-Winterthur Line, built 1948–57 by SLM.

Motor coach of the Vitznau–Rigi Railway of 1950–56.

motor coaches have the wheel-arrangements 1A-A1 with two motors of 163 hp each, 66 seats, and weight in working order of 26.5 tons. The driving trailer has 73 seats and weighs 11.3 tons. All the new vehicles are in modern, self-supporting, lightweight design. The length of the train is 31.3 m.

The Centovalli Railway, Switzerland

In 1959, the Centovalli Line of the FRT group received two modern three-unit trains; the Italian section ordered the same. The trains run over the 51-km-long Locarno–Domodossola Line providing improved service not only through this famous and beautiful Alpine valley but also between the west and south of Switzerland, shortening traveling time by 30 minutes. The vehicles were supplied by BBC (Technomasio Italiano) and Schindler, Pratteln; they have the following main dimensions:

Gauge: 1,000 mm
Total length of three-coach train: 34,000 mm
Bogie wheel base: 2,300 mm
Wheel diameter: 780 mm
Tare weight: 59 tons
Number of seats: 113
Current: 1,300-v, D.C.
1-hour output of the eight traction motors: 980 hp at 43.5 km/h
Maximum speed: 60 km/h

The three-coach train has four motorized bogies with two motors each; it is thus fully motorized. The train unit has three separate coach bodies, each supported on the bogies. The vehicles are built in modern steel self-supporting design.

The Bellinzona–Mesocco Railway, Switzerland

Crossing the Misoxer Valley (Mesolcina), this line opened in 1907 as the first railway in Europe to use 1,500-v D.C. and motor coaches for this current. It also was the first Swiss line to use high-tension direct current. The railway leads towards the San Bernardino Pass, has meter-gauge, and is about 31-km-long. Maximum gradient is 60‰ and the line climbs to 620 m.

Originally, five passenger and freight cars were ordered. All vehicles had four axles and were fully motorized. Two of the vehicles had 380 hp/1-hour output, the other four, 240 hp. The motors were arranged in pairs and could be used in series and parallel connection, as well as in shunt arrangement. The motor coaches weighed 11.15 and 10.9 tons. Total length was 15.1 and 11.1 m, with total wheel bases of 11.5 and 7.5 m. Driving wheel diameter was 20 km/h and maximum speed was 45 km/h.

In 1942, the line was amalgamated with the Rhaetian Railway and passenger services were replaced in 1972 by motor bus, an unusual action in Switzerland. The freight traffic remained on the rails.

Motorcoach train for the Centovalli Railway, 1959.

Bellinzona–Mesocco Railway motorcoach train.

Bellinzona–Mesocco Railway freight motor coach.

Motor coach of 1907 of the Valle Maggia Railway.

The Valle Maggia Railway, Switzerland

This private railway ran from Locarno to Ponte Brolla and Bignasco, in all 27.5-km-long, with meter-gauge and 33‰ gradients. It used 5,000-v 1-phase A.C. (20 Hz) and 800-v D.C. in the town district of Locarno. The three motor coaches had rod-collectors for side current collection.

The vehicles had two 2-axle bogies and four 40-hp motors, gear ratio was 13:67, and wheel diameter was 860 mm. Speeds were 45 km/h on level surfaces and 18 km/h on the 33‰ gradients. The electrical installations were supplied by MFO.

Other details were: weight, 27 tons; length, 16,000 mm; wheelbase, 10,000 mm. The line was changed to 1,200-v D.C. operation in 1925 to bring it in line with the Centovalli system, but by 1965 it needed complete renewal and in the absence of financial support was closed down.

The Hamburg–Altona–Blankenese–Ohlsdorf Lines, Germany

In 1907, the Prussian State Railways electrified the above-named lines near Hamburg, about 26.5-km-long, with single-phase A.C. of 6,300-v and 25 Hz. Fifty-four twin-motor coaches were ordered; each half had three axles, whereby the two outer axles

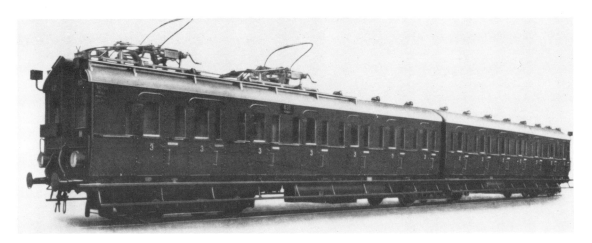

Altona–Blankenese–Ohlsdorf Line of the DR. Bo'-2'-2' motorcoach train supplied by BBC-Mannheim. The central "Jacobs" bogie is common to both vehicles.

formed a normal 2-axle bogie while the inner ones of both vehicles formed a "Jacobs" bogie, on which rested the coach body. One bogie had a single and the other had double Winter–Eichberg motors of 115 hp. Each twin-motor coach had a main transformer with two exciter transformers for the two and the one motor. Gear ratio was 1:4.22 and each duplex unit weighed 70 tons. The vehicles were supplied by AEG; in addition, six similar ones came from Siemens. BBC-Mannheim also participated in the work. The vehicles were 30,000 mm long and accommodated 97 passengers.

The Electrification of the Illinois Traction System, U.S.A.

From 1907, this line used electric traction on 146 kilometers with 3,300-v 1-phase A.C. of 25 Hz and with 600-v D.C. in towns. Ten motor cars were ordered, each with four 75-hp motors, supplied by General Electric. The line was converted to total 600-v D.C. in 1909. Motor tension is 250-v, and the vehicles are 17 m long and have 58 seats.

The Ritten or Renon Railway in Bozen/Bolzano, Italy

Bozen, nowadays called Bolzano, is the center of the Southern Tyrol. Until 1918 Austrian, it now belongs to Italy and is an important tourist center of the Dolomite Alps, famous for its wine trade and also the end of the Brenner Pass Railway. The railway up the Ritten Mountain, opened in 1908, was designed for rack-and-adhesion traffic. It had meter-gauge and was 12-km-long.

The line started at Bozen (265 m above sea level) and led to a high plateau at 1,250 m. The rack section was 4.1-km-long and had gradients of 250‰ using Strub's rack rail. Motor coaches and trailers

Motorcoach train of the Ritten (Renon) Railway, near Bozen (Bolzano), Italy.

Rack locomotive for Ritten Railway for rack section.

were employed, while on the rack section locomotives pushed the trains uphill. The difficult line, traversed in 80 minutes, used 800-v D.C. and had considerable passenger and freight traffic.

The Motor Coaches of the Loetschberg Railway and its Ancillary Lines, Switzerland

When the rolling stock was ordered in 1908 for the Spiez–Frutigen test line of the proposed Loetschberg Line, the order also comprised three 1-phase A.C. motor coaches. These were to be used for local traffic between Spiez and Frutigen, and later to Kandersteg.

The vehicles had two 2-axle bogies and driver's cabs at both ends. Vehicles supplied by Siemens were 20.3 m long, and one of the two bogies was fully motorized, using 8-pole nose-suspended motors. Hourly output was 230-hp per motor or 460-hp per vehicle, and gear ratio was 1:3.45, with a traveling speed of 45 km/h and a maximum speed of 70 km/h. Hourly tractive effort was 5,000 kg, with a maximum of 7,400 kg. Each motor coach could haul up to 240 tons on 15‰ gradients. The vehicles had two pantographs and a main transformer fixed under the main frame; there were 10 steps of the controller.

In 1935, all three motor coaches received new electrical equipment with four 200-hp motors; they were scrapped in 1954. Two vehicles also were ordered in 1925 that can be called either motor coaches or locomotives, CFe 2/6, since they consisted of a 3-axle engine part with a 500-hp motor, two driving and one running axle, and one short-coupled coach part with passenger and luggage compartments and a driver's cab. In 1956, the locomotive parts were rebuilt for service purposes.

In 1929, series CFe 4/5 motor coaches for passenger and luggage services were ordered. These later were rebuilt without the passenger compartments (De 4/5) and the nose-suspended motors were replaced by fully sprung units. One pantograph was removed and remote control was introduced in the first instance to run auto push-and-pull trains between Kandersteg and Goppenstein. Main dimensions of these vehicles were as follows: length, 20,900 mm; total wheelbase, 16,600 mm; driving wheel diameter, 1,048 mm; running wheel diameter, 850 mm; weight, 70–75 tons; 1-hour output, 1,600 hp; maximum speed, 90 km/h; gear ratio, 1:3.60/1:3.89; suppliers, SLM, SIG, MFO, and SAAS.

In 1935, BLS and the related lines started using lightweight vehicles. The line ordered five Ce 2/4 lightweight motor coaches that were supplied in

BLS motor coach for Spiez–Frutigen Section, 460 hp, 1910.

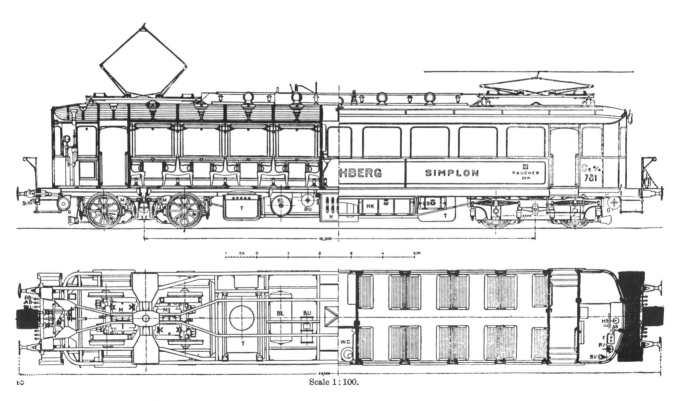

Diagram for BLS motor coach.

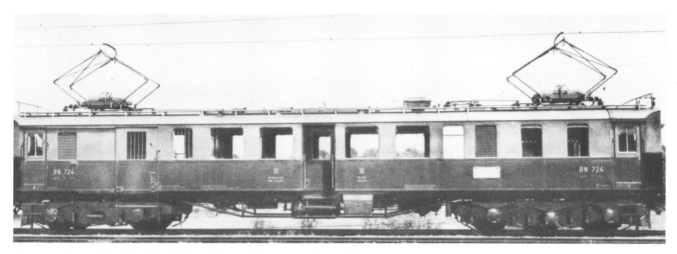

Motor coach type CFe 4/5 of the BLS and Berne–Neuenburg Line, 1929.

2'Bo'+Bo'2' twin motor coach of the BLS series ABDe 4/8 746–748 (later rebuilt).

three different variants; they all weighed about 35 tons and had a 1-hour rating of 300–400 hp with 90–100 km/h maximum speeds. In three of these vehicles, the transformer was situated on the roof because the low-slung design gave little space under the floor. In 1938, two more vehicles were ordered with 480-hp output and 110 km/h speed.

Two additional duplex lightweight train sets with double output followed at the same time. They contained first- and second-class compartments, luggage and mail parts, and had the serial number ABDZe 4/6. The two halves are coupled in the middle with a Jacobs bogie. Also for the line Berne–Schwarzenburg, a smaller twin-coach was ordered with 480-hp output and 80 km/h maximum speed. In 1944–45, three twin-motor, series ABDe 4/8

coaches were ordered that were similar to the previous ones, but had a more up-to-date layout and formed the basis for future vehicles.

In 1954 and 1957, BLS purchased five lightweight express motorcoach train sets—series ABDe 4/8, 746–750—from BBC, SAAS, SIG and SLM, which were of all-steel construction and were insulated with asbestos to control temperature and noise. Originally, the vehicles also were to operate under 3,000-v D.C. to allow for tourist traffic via the Simplon to Italy. The very simplified electrical installation comprises pantograph, transformer, and SAAS cam-operated contactor gear. Each train has four BBC motors (1-hour total output of 1,200 hp, later increased to 1,600 hp). The complete high tension installation is positioned in the roof or in a

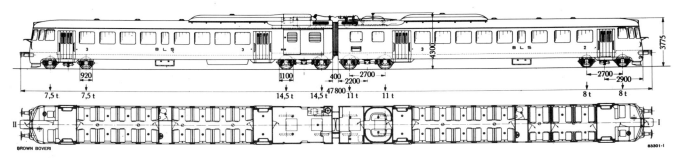

Schematic layout of twin motor coach.

compartment in the center of the train. Only the inner bogies are motorized, so as to have short, high-tension connections. The twin-motor coach train can haul a 50- to 60-ton trailing load with 75 km/h at 27‰. The bogies were originally of the torsion-bar type, later replaced by standard coach bogies, which increased speed from 110 to 125 km/h. Other main particulars were:

Wheel arrangement: 2-Bo+Bo-2
Total length: 47,800/47,300 mm
Total wheel base: 43,300 mm
Driving wheel diameter: 1,100 mm
Running wheel diameter: 910/920 mm
1-hour output: 1,600 hp at 75 km/h
Gear ratio: 1:4/27
Maximum speed: 110/125 km/h
Service weight: 84 tons/96 tons

A further development was the order of five motorcoach trains—ABDe 4/8, 751–755—in 1964. These vehicles have the same dimensions as the previously mentioned ones, but the weight in running order is 96 tons. The vehicles have a novel BBC rubberlink drive. There also are silicone recti-fiers and smoothing coils to avoid motor pulsations. The trains can run under multiple-unit or remote control.

As replacements for the heavyweight motor coach De 4/5, the railway in 1953–56 ordered three motor coaches—Be 4/4, 761–763—with a 1-hour output of 2,000 hp and a maximum speed of 110 km/h. They were then the most powerful single-motor coaches in existence and formed the basis for the express motor coaches RBe 4/4 of the SBB and similar ones for Swiss private lines.

Original (1908) motor coach for Rotterdam–Hague, Holland.

The Electric Motor Coaches for Rotterdam–Scheveningen and Later Dutch Efforts

The Dutch HSM Railway started to use electric traction in 1908 when the Rotterdam–Hague line extended in 1909 to Scheveningen. Originally, 850-v D.C. with a maximum speed of 55 km/h was to be used. In Holland at that time there were two competing railway companies, including the HSM. The railway finally decided to change its current system in view of the recent success of A.C. traction and to use the latter with 10,000-v 1-phase for the 33 kilometer line, increasing maximum speed to 90 km/h. The electrified rail length was 75 kilometers. The power station produced 5,000-v, 3-phase A.C. with 25 Hz, which was first transformed into 2-phase current and then into 10,000-v. The line was subdivided into two sections, with one phase supplying one section and the second phase handling the other. Between the two sections was a current-free 4-m-long wire.

The railway initially ordered 19 motor coaches and nine trailers; later, it added four of these well-designed and successful vehicles. Each bogie of the 4-axle motor coaches had one motor of 180 hp/1-hour, and each motor coach had two pantographs

Motorcoach train of NS, supplied by Metropolitan-Vickers.

Dutch motorcoach train set.

Postwar four-unit motorcoach set of NS supplied by Heemaf.

and two main switches. The electro-magnetic controller had eight steps connected to the main transformer in a ratio of 1:1; the purpose of the two transformers was to continue work if one failed. One of these original motor coaches is preserved in the Railway Museum in Utrecht. The vehicles were supplied by Beijnes and the electrical installation by Siemens.

The train consisted of two motor coaches and one or two middle trailers which could be run in multiple units. Gear ratio was 1:3, traveling speed was 60 km/h, and maximum speed was 100 km/h. Total length was 17,270 mm; bogie wheel base, 2,500 mm; distance of bogie pivots, 12,150 mm. The vehicles were very solidly and elegantly designed and had 56 to 88 seats. One empty motor coach weighed about 51 tons. For later Dutch developments, see page 101.

The Nonstal Railway from Trento (Trient) to Malles (Malé), Italy

This 60-km-long line was opened in 1909 with 800-v D.C. The railway serves the Nons Valley, a well-known and beautiful Alpine valley. Originally, 4-axle motor coaches were ordered with a weight of 21 tons. Each axle was driven, the gear ratio being 1:4.6. The

motors were 4-pole series-connected A.C. motors with pole-changing. They had 44 hp/1-hour output and 18-hp continuous output. Speed was regulated by series and parallel connections of the motors, together with field weakening. The electrical installations were supplied by AEG and Oe.SSW.

Twelve motor coaches were ordered initially with these main features: length, 13,500 mm; distance of bogie pivots, 6,700 mm; bogie wheel base, 2,000 mm; and wheel diameter, 900 mm. The vehicles had 36 seats, a luggage compartment and two drivers' cabs.

To cover the considerable freight traffic, the railway in 1911 ordered two freight motor coaches, which also had 2 x 2-axle bogies, weighed 19 tons tare, and could take a load of 8 tons. They were 13,200 mm long, bogie wheel base was 2,000 mm, and pivot distance was 6,500 mm. They were supplied by Graz Wagonworks and had the same electrical outfits as the passenger vehicles; later, the motors were changed to 66 hp/1-hour ones.

Traffic increased after World War II, and the narrow roads and the small railway no longer could cope with modern transportation conditions. It was decided to rebuild the line completely with 3,000-v D.C.; the line re-opened in 1955. Four new three-coach trains and three single-motor coaches were ordered.

Original (1909) motor coach of the Trient–Malé (Malles) Railway, Italy.

Freight motorcoach train for Trient–Malé Railway.

New motorcoach train for Trient–Malé Railway.

Modern BCFhe 4/4 motor coach for the Wengernalp Railway (Switzerland).

The Wengernalp Railway, Switzerland

This 19-km-long, 800-mm-gauge line is an all-rack railway with gradients between 250 and 180‰. The line, which uses Riggenbach rail and 1,500-v D.C., started with steam traction in 1893 and is considered the first attempt to bring a railway up the Jungfrau Mountains. Electrification took place in 1909. The line starts at Lauterbrunnen and goes from Grindelwald to the Kleine Scheidegg, a pass 2,061 m above sea level.

The original locomotives were replaced in 1948–58 by new vehicles—motor coaches ABFhe 4/4. The original 15 locomotives supplied by SLM/Alioth/BBC are still partly in use. However, most traffic since the renewal is provided by 18 motor coaches supplied by SLM/BBC, which can use up to two driving trailers, each train thus carrying 100 to 150 passengers. The vehicles have five different brake systems, tare weight is 23.5 tons, and they are 15,170 mm long. Electrical equipment consists of four 150 hp/1-hour motors equaling 600 hp/1-hour per coach. Speed when going uphill is 17 to 22 km/h, and running downhill it reaches 12 to 15 km/h. The vehicles have 44 seats and room for 10 standing passengers.

The Electrified Lines of the Southern Railway of England; later Southern Region of British Railways

The Southern Region of British Railways (formerly the Southern Railway) has claimed for 40 years that it operates the biggest electric railway system in the world—a claim that has never been disputed. London, one of the largest cities in the world with over 8 million inhabitants, has special and unique transportation problems.

The English love to have their own house and garden, and live as far away as possible from their work place. Thus, even the middle and working classes have their houses and gardens in the suburbs and the typical breadwinner of the family commutes every working day into London and home again,

Original Bo'-Bo' freight motor coach for the Southern Electrification with 6,000-v, 1-phase A.C. (England).

Bogie and motor for freight motor coach, Southern Electric.

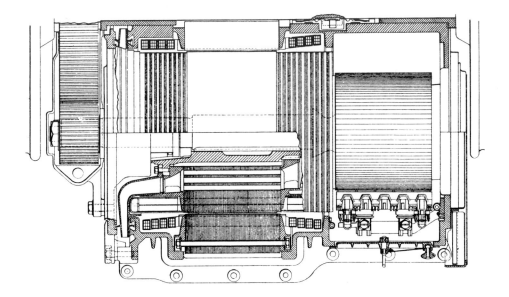

often traveling distances as great as 50 to 60 miles each way.

To accommodate large numbers of commuters, trains have eight to twelve coaches, all motorized, and train sequences often of 15 to 20 seconds. The lines have four or even six pairs of rails; most vehicles have side doors to all compartments to allow quick entry and exit. In such an intensive service, even small errors and interruptions can lead to serious delays that are only increased by the often very foggy weather conditions in England.

The Southern has five mainline stations in London, some with up to 23 platforms. Freight traffic is carried on mainly at night, when diesel, electro-diesel, and electric locomotives are used.

The first electrification efforts came in 1909 when an experimental line was opened between Peckham Rye and Battersea Park in South London and later extended to the Victoria and London Bridge terminals. The work was carried out under the direction of a very able engineer, Sir Philip Dawson, and used 6,600-v, 1-phase A.C.; the line belonged originally to a private company, the London, Brighton, and South Coast Railway. Another company was the London and South Western Railway, which electrified several lines out of Waterloo Station but used 600-v D.C. and third-conductor rail.

After the 123 private rail companies were amalgamated in 1923 into four companies, the entire southern network came under the Southern Railway. Electrification was continued, but all with 600-v D.C. and later 750-v and conductor rail. The A.C. system

also was converted, and, in 1946, 1,139 kilometers of line with 2,830 kilometers of rail were electrified.

The London Brighton and South Coast Railway used motor coaches with side corridors in chocolate and cream color, forming trains of one 4-axle motor coach and one 4-axle trailer. Motor coaches were fully equipped with four 150-hp motors. They had two bow collectors that were designed as duplex current collectors to be used in each direction. One two-vehicle train had 112 seats in third class and 12 in first class.

Because the electric system was a great success, it was decided in 1911 to extend the system to the important mainline, London–Clapham Junction–Crystal Palace–Streatham Hill–Selhurst. This line had a very narrow profile, especially in tunnels, and thus needed especially narrow vehicles, type CZ. The trains consisted of end-driving trailers with the center coach motorized. Such a train had 170 third-class and 36 first-class seats.

The second electrification program was that of the London and South Western Railway, which had followed U.S. practice and had used 600-v D.C. The work was carried out by British Westinghouse (later sold to Metropolitan-Vickers). A total of 252 vehicles were ordered, which ran in three-car trains consisting of two (outer) motor coaches and a middle trailer. For rush-hour services, two such trains were coupled with two trailers between forming an eight-car train. Each motor coach had two 275-hp motors; that is, four per three-coach unit. These three-coach trains were 47,000 mm long, had 190 seats, and

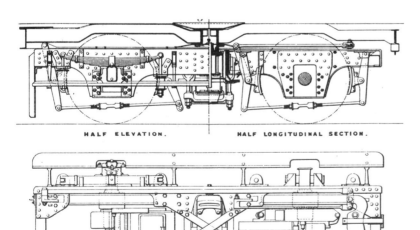

HALF ELEVATION.   HALF LONGITUDINAL SECTION.

Another bogie and motor for freight motor coach, Southern Electric.

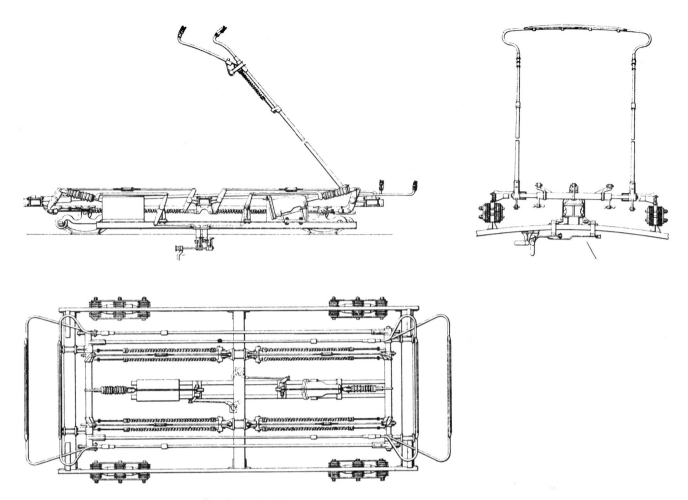

Pantograph for freight motor coach, Southern Electric.

Southern Railway motorcoach set.

weighed 94 tons. The nose-suspended motors were mounted directly in the leading bogie, and the control installations were mounted at the back of the cab directly above the bogie. The controller was easily accessible from a mail and luggage compartment behind it. The vehicles had even a kind of remote control. These early vehicles formed the basis for later designs.

After World War I, the electrification program was recommenced in 1923 when the newly created Southern Railway took over the work. Although the 1-phase A.C. system with overhead catenary was extended by 150 kilometers to improve traffic conditions, it already had been decided to change the whole system to 600-v D.C. and third rail.

New vehicles were ordered that were unusual: a five-coach train consisted of two leading and two trailing cars with cabs at each end, while the center vehicle was a kind of luggage motor van that contained the whole electrical installation. This 4-axle vehicle from Metropolitan-Vickers had the following technical details: 101 coaches were delivered, of which 21 were luggage-motor-vans; these were 12,810 mm long, had a 1,093 mm wheel diameter, bogie wheel base was 2,462 mm, and they weighed 62 tons. There were four 250-hp motors, together with main and auxiliary transformers. Coaches had two air-operated bow collectors. The trailers were 15,730 mm long and weighed 24 to 25 tons. The total five-coach train had 304 seats.

After 1925, the system was changed gradually to 600-v D.C. and third rail, and in 1932–33 it reached Brighton and Worthing, two important seaside resorts.

Southern Railway four-unit suburban motorcoach set.

"Brighton Belle" Pullman train for Southern Railway.

Among various vehicles that were ordered was the famous Pullman train, "Brighton Belle." This was the first all-steel motorcoach train, and it aroused great interest. It had five vehicles consisting of one driving motor coach, one third-class trailer, two first-class trailers, and a final driving motor coach, with cabs at both ends of the train. The train was luxuriously equipped and weighed 249 tons. It had room for 152 third-class and 40 first-class passengers.

For the slow and fast suburban services, 33 four-coach trains were ordered, which weighed 139 tons and offered room for 274 passengers. In all, 285 vehicles were supplied, of which 38 were Pullman coaches.

The electrifications that took place after World War II brought the totals to 1,139 kilometers of line and 2,830 kilometers of rail; tension was increased to 750-v D.C.

It is an almost impossible task to describe the history of the Southern Electric in a few lines. Even a substantial handbook could hardly tell the fascinating and complete story of the largest suburban network in the world.

Vehicles ordered in 1956 brought certain developments to their final point. This development occurred on the so-called Kent–Coast electrification, which consisted of two plans that foresaw the changeover to electric traction of 285-kilometer rail and 210-kilometer line length. Many lines were quadrupled and platforms lengthened to take longer trains. The vehicles to be acquired were built by the railway company itself, English Electric supplying the electrical parts. The order comprised 53 four-coach trains that consisted of a motor coach with one motorized bogie, two trailers, and a non-motorized driving trailer. The motors were four 250-hp nose-suspended types, and speed control was by cam-operated contactor gear.

In the sixties, additional orders were placed primarily to improve running qualities. For example, roller bearings were introduced, and 10 freight motor coaches were ordered to be used for "boat trains" to the Channel ports. They were 20,435 mm long and weighed 47 tons. They contained two driver's cabs and luggage and personnel compartments. There were two 250-hp EEC motors in addition to a motor generator and battery to run over nonelectrified sections; they could haul 100-ton trailing loads and also could be used for postal and parcel services. A pair of four-vehicle trains of two-story coaches were also tried (they weighed 136 tons and had 1,104 seats), but they were unsuccessful with the traveling public.

The Midi of France: Electrification of its Line Perpignan–Villefranche-de-Conflet

This line is 47-km-long, has gradients of 21.4‰ and is a continuation of the Pyrénées Railway, also meter-gauge. Electrification took place in 1910 and some interesting locomotives and motor coaches were ordered. Electric traction started in 1913 using 30 A.C. motor coaches supplied by Dyle and Balalon and Westinghouse. They had the following main data: weight, 60 tons; length, 19,140 mm; total wheel base, 15,180 mm; bogie wheel base, 2,540 mm; wheel diameter, 1,020 mm; four motors of 125 hp/1-hour; gear ratio, 20:63; maximum speed, 85 km/h; 44 seats. In addition, 13 trailers were ordered. Fourteen of the original vehicles are still used for A.C. traffic, while 13 were rebuilt for D.C. and two came first to the SBB and then to the Vereinigte Hutwiler Bahnen.

The Bernina Railway, Switzerland

This line is 60.8-km-long, meter-gauge, and has maximum gradients of 70‰. It is very unusually designed because it crosses the 2,257-mm Bernina Pass in the open without a tunnel during full winter services. The line connects St. Moritz in the Engadine with Tirano in the Veltlin. Today it is part of the Rhaetian Railway network.

Building took place from 1908 to 1910, and the line was electrified with 750-v (later 1,000-v) D.C. and catenary. Originally, 14 BCe 4/4 motor coaches were ordered and also one Fe 2/2 freight motor coach. The first series had four driven axles in two bogies, having 2,000 mm wheel base. Weight was 28.1 tons; length, 13,910 mm; total wheel base, 10,000 mm; and wheel diameter, 850 mm. The four motors have an output of 75 hp/1-hour; gear ratio is 1:4.5; and maximum speed is 45 km/h. The freight motor coach weighed 12.5 tons, was 7,150 mm long, and had 850 mm-diameter wheels. In 1911, two lightweight, 2-axle locomotives and three motor coaches with additional luggage compartments—series BCFe 4/4—were added.

After amalgamation with the Rhaetian Railways, many motor coaches were modernized between 1946 and 1956. They received 130–145 hp/1-hour motors, and some can run on the 2,200-v Chur–Arosa Line. To enable the line to fulfill ever-increasing demands, new vehicles were supplied by BBC/SAAS/SWS from 1964 to 1973. These new motor coaches are of self-supporting, all-steel con-

Original BCe 4/4 motorcoach train of the Bernina Railway, 1910.

Original and rebuilt motor coach of the Bernina Railway, now also used on Chur–Arosa line.

struction with modern, luxurious layout. Main data are: type ABe 4/4; length, 16,540 mm; pivot center distance, 11,000 mm; bogie wheel base, 2,200 mm; wheel diameter, 920 mm; weight, 43 tons. There are four motors of 230 hp/1-hour. They can haul 60 tons of trailing load on a 70‰ gradient.

The Tatra Railway, Czechoslovakia

The line Poprad–Tatra to Strbske Pleso was built in 1911 and opened with electric traction. The line has meter-gauge and leads to the foothills of the High Tatra mountains. There are two types of motor coaches, EM 48 of 1911 and EM 49 of 1931–1950. The railway carries considerable passenger traffic and is used mainly for tourist and winter sport traffic. In 1965, 18 new, three-coach, articulated train sets were ordered.

The Jungfrau Railway, Switzerland

The Jungfrau Railway was opened in sections between 1898 and 1912. It is the highest mountain line of Europe (3,451 m) and originally used only rack locomotives. New motor coach trains were ordered after 1954 that increased traveling speed on the valley sections from 18 to 24 km/h and on the steep mountain sections (100–250 percent) from 9 to 12 km/h, thus reducing traveling time from 54 to 42 minutes. The 3-phase A.C. tension was increased from 650- to 1,125-v and frequency from 40 to 50 Hz.

The ten new trains ordered from SLM/BBC/ SWS consisted of a motor coach and a driving trailer. The trains are 29,000 mm long, the motor coach is 14,795 mm, and one train has 108 seats and room for 35 standing passengers, as well as a small luggage compartment.

The narrow cross-section of the line made it very difficult to install the motor into one bogie. The floor of the vehicle is only 700 mm above railhead and the roof is 2,910 mm. There is only one driver's cab—on the valley side—carrying all switchgear on its rearwall. There is only one 600-hp, 4-pole, 3-phase asynchrone slipping motor. This motor transmits power to two driven axles and two rack wheels. The latter are freely movable on their axis.

There is a rack-wheel operated by hand or solenoid connected to the emergency brake and "deadman" control. The motor is controlled by a cam-operated automatic switching gear that changes to regenerative braking when running downhill. The train also can roll downhill without current, whereby the stator is excited by D.C. and the brake energy is brought to the roof resistances.

Main data are as follows: wheel arrangement, Bo-2, Strub rack rail; 1-hour tractive effort, 13,500 kg/11.4 km/h or 6,750 kg at 22.8 km/h; maximum speeds, (uphill) 22.8 km/h, (downhill) 25 km/h; maximum tractive effort, 17,600/8,800 kg; driving wheel diameter, 668 mm; gear ratios, 1:12.61/1:6.31; weights, (laden) 45 tons, (tare) 23.5 tons.

Jungfrau Railway: 1912 rack locomotive and train.

Jungfrau Railway: 1955 motorcoach train.

The Electric Motor Coaches of the Paris–Orléans Railway of France and Later Vehicles of the SNCF

The first deliveries of electric motor coaches or motorcoach trains for the Paris–Orléans Line were faithful copies of U.S. vehicles. From 1912 to 1937 (when the railways were nationalized), a considerable number and varied types of vehicles were supplied both for 700- as well as 1,500-v D.C. lines. Most vehicles could run in multiple-unit operation but took no trailers.

In 1932, 1,000-hp motor coaches were built that weighed 74 tons, followed by two designs for the electrification of Paris–Le Mans in 1937. One was designed for fast intercity traffic and formed the basis for the vehicles supplied during the next 25 years. These were twin-units, resting on three bogies. The vehicles were built in stainless steel by Carel-Fouché-Budd. All axles were motorized by nose-suspended 240-hp motors, giving a total output of 1,440 hp per train. Maximum speed was 130 km/h and, on tests, one train reached 186 km/h. Tare weight was 76 tons.

The second design was a suburban train, delivered by Somua that had two 2-axle bogies, all motorized. These weighed 38.5 tons, were 23,000 mm long, and had a 1-hour output of 850 hp and a maximum speed of 140 km/h. A test vehicle reached 170 km/h. These vehicles also could be used in multiple-unit control and took no trailers.

In 1939, three newer types appeared. One of these was an electro-diesel coach that experimentally could be used under 1,500-v D.C. and also had a 440-hp diesel motor so it could be run on non-electrified sections.

Another type was a train of motor coaches for 600/700-v suburban services. These were built by Michelin for conductor-rail services and had rubber-covered tires. They were used on the St. Germain Line. The simple vehicle was very successful, and had very good acceleration and braking characteristics. From a speed of 140 km/h, it could be stopped in 9.5 seconds in a 140-m distance. Output was 776 hp at 675-v and 120 km/h.

The coach weighed only 32 tons. Maximum speed was 115 km/h. It offered capacity for 136

Motorcoach train Z.5100/ZS.15100 for suburban services of Paris (Melun and Chartres) made from stainless steel and built in 1954.

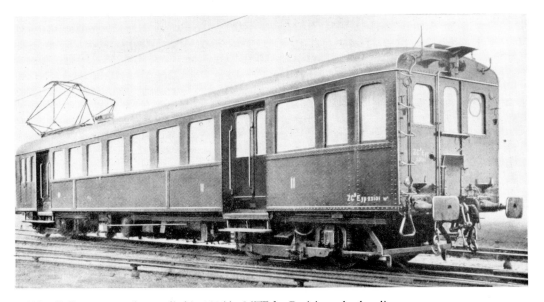

1,500-v D.C. motor coach, supplied in 1924 by MTE for Parisian suburban lines.

sitting and 120 standing passengers. In addition, there was a luggage compartment. Total length of the three-unit train was 38,080 mm. The three parts were connected concertina-fashion, and there were four 4-axle bogies. Each bogie had one motor that drove both inner axles and was fixed in the frame. Drive from motor to axle was by Cardan-shaft and universal coupling.

In 1960, the long-distance express trains of series 7100 appeared. These have four units with one motor coach, one driving trailer, and two center trailers. Thirty-three such trains were ordered from Decauville, De Dietrich, and MFO. The motor coach has a driving bogie with two motors and a running bogie. They have two pantographs, and the driving trailer has an outer-driven bogie, again with two motors. Other main features are: length, 26,100 mm; weight, 53 tons; 70 seats and 39 standing passengers; 1-hour output; 1,300 hp; maximum speed, 120 km/h. The trains were to be used on the Lyon–Béziers route.

In 1957, four prototype vehicles were ordered for 50-Hz traction for the Paris suburban services. They have serial numbers Z.9056–9. Each train has a

Twin motor coach for Parisian suburban lines. Supplied in 1937 by Carel, Fouché, & CIE.

Suburban motor coach of the SNCF Paris–Ouest section, built in 1938 by Alsthom; 1,500-v D.C., 825 hp, 38-ton weight.

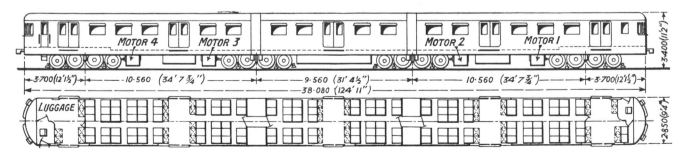

Current rail vehicle of 1939 for SNCF's Paris suburban lines with Michelin rubber-tired wheels.

Motorcoach train of the SNCF, series Z.7100, with three trailers, 1,500-v D.C., and 1,310 hp. Built by MFO, Décauville, and Diétrich.

SNCF 1,020 hp motorcoach train for 25,000-v, 1-phase A.C. 50 Hz. Series Z.9056–60. Built by Alsthom and a group of French manufacturers.

motor coach, trailer, and driving trailer, all built in stainless steel. Three of the vehicles have "mono-motor" bogies, two have germanium rectifiers, and one has a silicone rectifier (the bogie design is similar to the one for the well-known locomotive type BB 9400). Train No. Z.9058 has a 1-phase commutator motor with rotating transformer and auto-electronic speed control from the start to the desired speed, so that the driver only has to select the desired speed. The bogie is similar to the one for locomotive type BB 16500.

Main data of these vehicles are: length of three-coach unit, 74,450 mm; total weight, 108 to 112 tons; maximum speed, 120 to 100 km/h; 1-hour output, 750/685 kw; 256 sitting and 142 standing passengers.

Also in 1959, two 50-hp motor coaches with numbers Z.9060–1 were ordered for long-distance traffic. They have two motor bogies and silicone rectifiers. One motor coach can haul three trailers. Main data are 26,100-mm length; 58-ton weight; 120-km/h maximum speed; 965 kw/1-hour output; 70 seats and 79 stand spaces.

The Chur–Arosa Railway (now part of the Rhaetian Railway), Switzerland

This line leads through a most wild and desolate area of the Alps, with no less than 18 tunnels and 35 bridges or viaducts over a 10-m length. The difference in height is 1,154 m on 25.6-kilometers of line between Chur and Arosa, 12.4 kilometers in curves. Maximum gradient is an amazing 60‰.

The meter-gauge line was opened in 1914 using 2,000-v D.C., now 2,200-v. In 1925, four motor coaches were ordered and another one was ordered in 1929. The original vehicles have the following main dimensions: length, 17,500 mm; bogie wheel base, 2,400 mm; total wheel base, 12,750 mm; wheel diameter, 920 mm; 40 seats; four motors of 95 hp/1-hour at 21.3 km/h; ratio, 1:5.13; maximum speed, 25 km/h; weight 38.9 tons; and electrical part, 12.2 tons. The vehicles had wooden bodies, steel frames, and two bogies. They had vacuum and rail brakes. There are two cabs, four passenger compartments, and a luggage and mail compartment. In the center is the high-tension chamber. The motor coach was supplied by BBC/SWS. The four motors are of the nose-suspended type. There is a cam-operated contactor with eleven running and six braking steps; there are also two pantographs and a main switch.

In 1942, the line amalgamated with the Rhaetian Railway. After World War II, traffic increased substantially and very powerful motor coaches were ordered from SWS/BBC. They have the following main data: length, 17,700 mm; pivot distance, 11,350 mm; bogie wheel base, 255 mm; wheel diameter, 920 mm; 1-hour output of the four motors, 4 x 170 hp, with 60-ton trailing load and 27 km/h; weight, 43 tons.

After the amalgamation, five Bernina motor coaches were rebuilt so they also could be used on the Chur–Arosa Line. In 1957–58, six new motor coaches were ordered; another two similar ones were ordered in 1973.

Leuk–Leukerbad-Bahn, Switzerland

This meter-gauge line was electrified with 1,500-v D.C., and was 10-km-long with a 5-kilometer rack-line, having ABT's rack system. Maximum gradient was 160‰ and there was a difference in height of 771 m. Opened in 1915, there were three BCFe 4/4 motor coaches, with a 1-hour output of 680 hp. Maximum speed was 25 km/h on adhesion and 9 km/h on rack. The line was not renewed and closed in 1967.

1914 motor coach for Chur–Arosa Line, series BCFe 4/4 (see also Rhaetian and Bernina Lines).

Two motor coaches with trailers for Chur–Arosa Line; 4 x 275 hp, 43.4-ton weight. Built by BBC, SAAS, SWS.

1915 motorcoach train for Leuk–Leukerbad Railway.

Developments from 1914 to 1939
by Country and Railway;
Further Developments from
1939 to Present

The Zugspitz Railway in Bavaria, West Germany

The Zugspitze is the highest mountain in Germany (2,946 m) and, with its imposing and beautiful mountain scenery, has long been a center of tourism and mountaineering. For many years, plans had existed to build a rack-and-adhesion line to the top of the mountain. Very active in these efforts were an Austrian engineer, Josef Cathrein, and a well-known Swiss expert, Dr. Zehnder-Spoerry. However, their efforts failed, largely because of lack of capital.

In 1928, new efforts were made in which the AEG firm took over responsibility for building the line and making the electrical installations. It also provided two-fifths of the capital; the remainder was found by the newly created railway company. The meter-gauge line starts at Garmisch–Partenkirchen and then goes via Riessersee to Eibsee and to the so-called Platt; from this spot a cable-railway leads to the top. On the Platt, a large hotel named Schnee-Ferner-Haus was erected.

The line runs from Riffel Riss to the terminal in a 4,466-m long tunnel (including a reversing tunnel) and overcomes a distance in height of 1,000 m. The line goes by adhesion to Grainau, where locomotives are changed and the railway uses Riggenbach rack rail to the top. It was opened in 1930 and first used two types of locomotives, whose details are given in Table 7.

Railway authorities were opposed from the beginning to motor coach traffic on the mountain

Rack motor coach for the
Zugspitz Railway of Bavaria.

Table 7
ZUGSPITZ RAILWAY

	Adhesion Locomotive	Rack Locomotive
Wheel arrangement	Bo	Bo + 3Z
Weight (tons)	27	28
Maximum tractive effort (kg)	6,000	15,000
Maximum speed (km/h)	50	9
Driving wheel diameter (mm)	1,200	796
Running wheel diameter (mm)	————	600
Wheelbase (mm)	3,200	3,500
Length (mm)	6,900	6,300

section because they feared an ineffective and irregular braking effort. In 1954, however, a 4-axle motor coach was supplied by MAN/AEG, with SLM-Winterthur providing the rack drive. There are four driven axles. The four motors have an output of 144 kw each. Main details are: length, 13,800 mm; bogie center distance, 7,300 mm; bogie wheel base, 2,650 mm; weight, 22 tons; 95-passenger seating capacity.

Standard-Gauge Motor Coaches and Motorcoach Trains of the Swiss Federal Railways

The SBB started using motor coaches on the Swiss main and branch line services in 1923. For example, the motorcoach trains were used on the lines Geneva–Lausanne, Lausanne–Villeneuve, Berne–Thun, Basle–Olten, and Zurich–Meilen–Rapperswil.

In the course of the first electrification program, 46 motor coaches were ordered, 21 for passenger services and 25 for goods and parcel services. They had the serial numbers Ce 4/6, Ce 4/4, and Fe 4/4. All vehicles had their electrical equipment supplied by SAAS with coach parts by Schlieren and Neuhausen. The operation, with contactor gear, allowed multiple-unit control; all vehicles also had a deadman installation.

Motor coach Ce 4/6 (later Be 4/6) of the SBB, in its original state, 1923–26. Built by SAAS, SIG, SWS.

Six-axle bogie for motor coach
Ce 4/6.

Contactor gear for motor coach
Ce 4/6.

Motor coaches could be used singly or with trailers as well as in multiple-unit service with two motor coaches. Push-and-pull trains had a driving trailer at one end. From the start, the vehicles gave very satisfactory service and achieved daily runs up to 440 kilometers. Main dimensions of these vehicles are found in Table 8.

In the beginning, two Ce 4/4 vehicles had driving motors bought from the French Midi Railway, which later were replaced by new ones.

The vehicles described in Table 8 underwent various changes. For example, between the years 1961 and 1966, most of the Ce 4/6 and some Fe 4/4 (today numbered Be 4/6 and De 4/4) received new

steel bodies and modern braking systems; the bogies were improved by introducing rubber-spring supports. They also received new multiple-unit controls and the oil-operated main switch was replaced by an air-operated one; also, the second pantograph was removed. Vehicle number Be 4/6 was the test unit for these alterations and still has its original form, together with the original multiple-unit control and contactor gear.

Series Fe 4/4 also underwent some changes: between 1930 and 1939, eight vehicles received new transmission gears of 1:4.235 gear ratio, maximum speed was fixed at 75 km/h, and a recuperative braking system was introduced. Between 1948 and

Table 8
SWISS FEDERAL RAILWAYS

	Serial No. *Ce 4/6*	*Serial No.* *Ce 4/4*	*Serial No.* *Fe 4/4*
Number built	19	2	25
Numbers of motors	4	4	4
1-hour output (hp)	800	500	1,000
Driving wheel diameter (mm)	1,040	1,040	1,040
Gear ratio	1:3.65	1:3.15	1:4.235/ 1:3.60
Total length (mm)	20,000	17,500	15,200
Total weight (tons)	86	60	64
Weight of electrical part	27	23	26.6

Freight motor coach Fe 4/4 of the SBB, 1,000 hp.

Roof-mounted brake resistances for motor coach Fe 4/4.

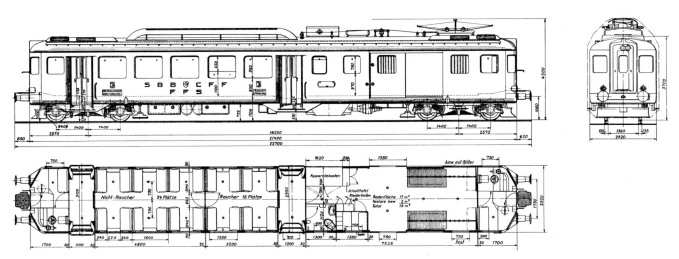

Schematic layout of Bo'-Bo' passenger and freight motor coach, series BDe 4/4 (was formerly CFe 4/4), 1952–54 of the SBB.

Bo'-Bo' passenger and freight motor coach, series BDe 4/4.

1958, new 1,100-hp motors were installed, and between 1966 and 1971, the wooden bodies were partly replaced by steel ones. The serial number was altered to De 4/4 and various improvements were made in the control installations.

Between 1953 and 1954, vehicles numbered 1681–1684 received MFO rubber-ring drive; the MFO spring-drive also was tested. However, the limited space hindered a successful construction and, later on, SAAS spring-drive was introduced.

In the years 1952 to 1954, 30 motor coaches of series BDe 4/4 were purchased from the firms of SWS, BBC, MFO, and SAAS for use with light trains on branch lines. Main dimensions were as follows: total length, 22,700 mm; total wheel base, 19,100 mm; wheel diameter, 940 mm; weight in working

order, 54 tons; 1-hour output, 1,600 hp; maximum speed, 100 and later 110 km/h; maximum tractive effort, 10,000 kg; 1-hour tractive effort at 70 km/h, 6,160 kg; gear ratio, 1:3.26.

From 1965 to 1967, three-coach trains were ordered, series RABDe 12/12, whereby up to four trains (12 vehicles) can be driven from one cab. All axles are motorized and the trains are used for the substantial suburban traffic between Zurich and Rapperswil. The trains have electronic speed control to adjust speed automatically and independently of the line profile. The trains are equipped with recuperative brakes and have two transformers, each supplying current to six motors. Technical data are as follows: total length of train, 73,300 mm; total wheel base, 69,300 mm; wheel diameter, 850 mm;

2,800 hp express motor coach, series RBe 4/4, of the SBB, 1959.

weight in working order, 170 tons; total 1-hour output, 3,320 hp; 1-hour tractive effort, 11,200 kg at 80 km/h; maximum tractive effort, 24,400 kg; gear ratio, 1:2.913; builders, SWS, FFA and SAAS.

A further type of motor coach is series RBe 4/4, which was supplied from 1959 to 1966 in 82 units. This series was first ordered in six prototypes for use in intercity traffic. Details are as follows: wheel arrangement, Bo'-Bo'; total length, 23,700 mm; total wheel base, 19,600 mm; driving wheel diameter, 1,040 mm; total weight, 64 to 68 tons; 1-hour output, 2,720 hp; 1-hour tractive effort at 80.4 km/h, 9,160

kg; gear ratio, 1:2.74; maximum speed, 125 km/h; builders, MFO and BBC, SIG and SWS.

The Lightweight Motor Coaches of the SBB: Series CLe 2/4 (later RAe 2/4 and RBe 2/4); also RAe 4/8 (RBe 4/8) and RABDe 12/12

Forced by the ever-increasing competition of the automobile and the economic crisis, many railway administrations and business firms in the thirties

Lightweight motor coach CLe 4/4 of the SBB.

realized that the land transport monopoly they had enjoyed for nearly 100 years was coming to an end. Light-weight vehicles were considered as a means to improve services and gain a competitive edge with fast, inexpensive intercity connections.

These lightweight vehicles were the exact opposite of the traditional design ideas of railway vehicles. They were to disregard classes and luggage, and they were to reduce cost by one-man control with the driver collecting tickets. They were to be built more economically, reduce running costs, and increase speed by easy starting. Consequently, they had to use special steels, lightweight alloys, and plastics. They were to allow quick entry and exit, thus requiring automatic opening and closing of doors. They were to have modern and attractive inside and outside layouts. In the electrical parts, there was to be only one pantograph, simple roof main switch, simpli-

fication of electrical installations above the bogies, and novel safety devices for the seated driver.

The SBB, together with the firm of Brown, Boveri and Cie, developed such a vehicle. It consisted of a low-positioned body seated on a "cranked" chassis between two 2-axle bogies. These bogies had a 2,500-mm wheelbase and carried the 21,500-mm-long body. Total wheelbase was 18,800 mm. Electrical installations were placed in two front compartments of low position and the whole vehicle was streamlined or air-smoothed; it was soon proved that streamlining reduced air resistance substantially. The vehicle had room for 70 sitting and 30 standing passengers. One of the bogies was a running one while the other contained the transformer and had both axles motorized.

It was intended from the start to use higher speeds, which meant the replacement of the axle-

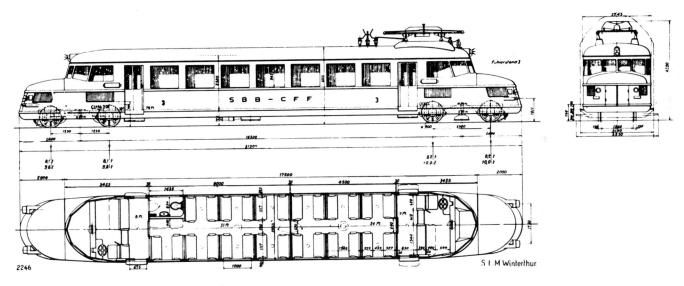

Schematic layout for motor coach CLe 4/4.

Welded body and frame structure for motor coach CLe 4/4.

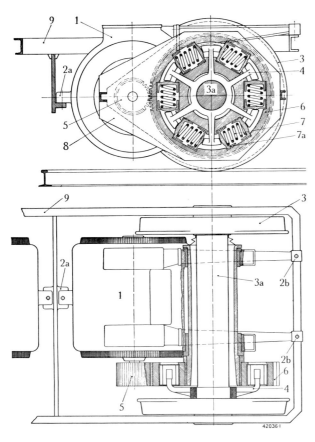

Motor drive for motor coach CLe 4/4.

Motorcoach train RBCFe 8/12 of the SBB, 1939.

hung motors by a motor with flexible power transmission. Brown Boveri developed a spring-link drive for this purpose. The motor transmits its power by a gear drive, the larger gear wheel sitting on a hollow shaft, and then works by star-shaped links attached to the driving axle so that relative movements between frame and axle are taken up by the gliding arm of the driving star.

Output of the two motors was 173 hp/1-hour or 150 hp at constant speed. Transmission ratio was 1:2.96 with 900-mm driving wheels. The air-cooled

transformer has an output of 210 KVA. Instead of a main switch there is a fully earthed roof fuse. In addition to the usual hand and air brakes, there is also a D.C. short-circuit brake. The roof is hollow and contains the brake resistances. The vehicle is controlled by an electropneumatic contactor gear. For one-man use, a BBC safety-control was provided.

Other main data are as follows: maximum speed, 125 km/h; weight of mechanical part; 20.7 tons; weight of electrical part, 12.1 tons; adhesive weight, 20 tons.

Sécherôn individual axle drive for motorcoach train RBCFe 8/12.

Driving controller for motorcoach train RBCFe 8/12.

Express twin motor coach of the SBB, series RBe 4/8.

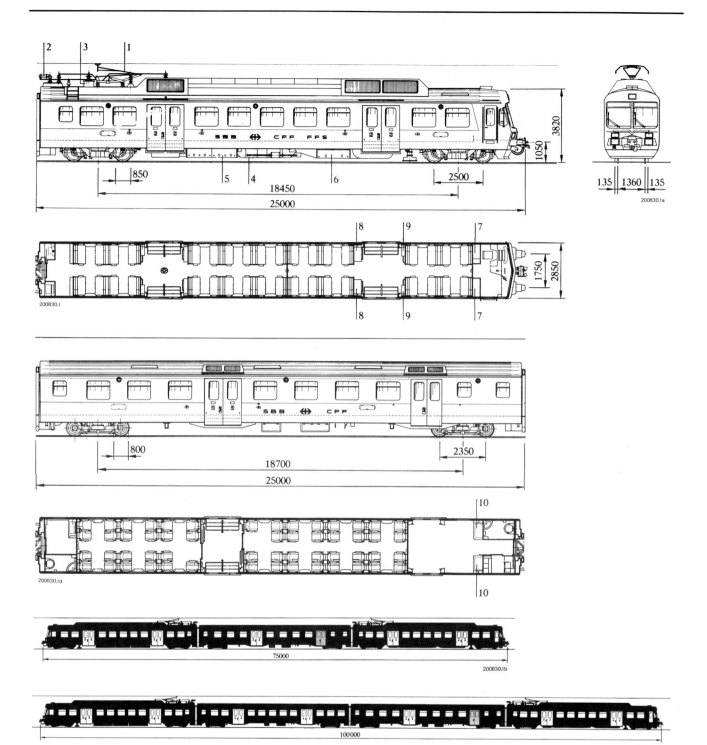

Suburban motor-coach composition, RABDe 8/16

1. Current collector
2. Airblast circuit-breaker
3. Surge diverter
4. Transformer
5. Equipment box

6. Box containing electronic firing system
7. Equipment cabinets with electronic control and regulating systems
8. Air duct for transformer and rectifier cooling
9. Air duct for traction motor cooling
10. Motor-coach equipment for continuous automatic train control (LZB)

Schematic layout of motorcoach train RABDe 12/12, SBB.

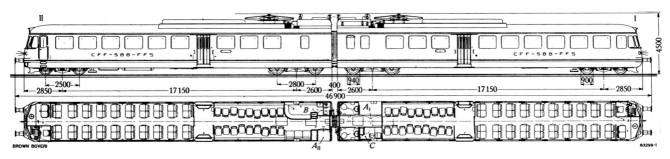

Schematic layout of express twin motor coach, series RBe 4/8.

Motor coach for RABDe 12/12 of the SBB.

The first vehicles, supplied in 1935, were numbered CLe 2/4 201. The motor coaches soon proved that they were not suited for intercity traffic or for stopping-train services, but they were a great success in tourist traffic and in heavy intercity services. There they were succeeded by triple units, RBCFe 8/12, but even these proved insufficient. Later lightweight motor coaches were built with normal coupling gear, which found good use on branch lines with trailer services.

The motorcoach trains RBe 4/8, later RAe 4/8, built in three units and two different variants for tourist traffic, had the following main data: wheel arrangement, 2'Bo' + Bo'2'; total length, 46,200/46,900 mm; total wheel base, 43,100/42,400 mm; wheel diameter, 940/900 mm; and weight in working order, 93/88 tons. There are four motors with a 1-hour output of 1,140/1,180 hp at 115.5/98 km/h. The relative tractive efforts are 2,650/3,800 kg, with maximum tractive effort of 4,600/7,000 kg. Transmission gear ratios are 1:2.64/1:3.26. Maximum speed is 150/125 km/h. Suppliers were SLM, SWS, and MFO, BBC, and SAAS.

Introduced in 1959 with 118 to 123 seats, these vehicles were the results of extensive research and testing efforts, which showed that remarkably increased performance could be achieved with them and series RABDe 12/12, introduced from 1965 to 1967. These results were achieved largely through weight reduction and improved starting and braking efforts. The three-component trains also are described in Chapter One.

The Rhaetian Railway, Switzerland

This is probably the most important narrow-gauge railway of Europe, having 1,000-mm gauge and 394-kilometer length. With maximum gradients of 70‰, the line was electrified beginning in 1919 and uses 11,000-v, single-phase A.C. of 16⅔ cycles.

Motor coach ABFe 4/4 of the Rhaetian Railways (Chur–Arosa Line), 1955–57.

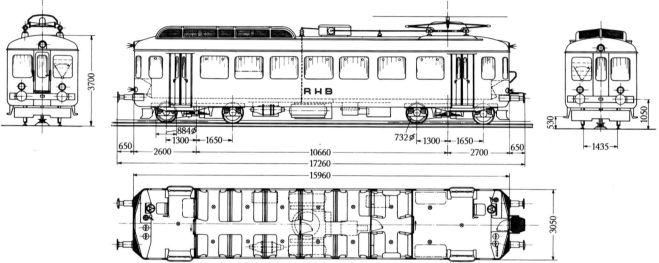

Schematic layout for motor coach ABFe 4/4.

The railway primarily serves the canton of Grison (Graubuenden), whose area of 7,113 sq km makes it the largest canton in Switzerland in size but the smallest in population with only 19 inhabitants per square kilometer. Grison shows the greatest contrasts in landscape as well as climate from the other cantons. Oranges and lemons grow in the valleys, but in the Bernina group of mountains, 4,055 m above sea level, large glaciers are predominant. The area contains such famous holiday, health, and sport resorts as St. Moritz, Davos, Arosa, and Pontresina, which came within reach of mankind only with the arrival of the railway.

The first line, opened with steam traction in 1888, was the Landquart–Davos section. The terrain difficulties of the 394-km-long network required 117 tunnels (38-km-long) and 487 bridges and viaducts (12-km-long in all). The main lines, as already mentioned, are electrified with 11,000-v, 1-phase A.C. of $16\frac{2}{3}$ Hz, but some lines use different currents, such as the Bernina Line, 1,000-v D.C.; Misox 1,500-v D.C.; and Chur (Coire)–Arosa, 2,000-v D.C. (see separate descriptions). The locomotives have been described in another volume but there are five motorcoach types, as follows:

ABe 4/4—501–504, (1939–40)
Be 4/4—511–514, (1971)
ABDe 4/4—481–488, (1957–73)
BDe 4/4—491
ABe 4/4—41–49, (1964–72)

Type 1 has a 1-hour output of 588 hp with 37 tons laden weight and a 65 km/h maximum speed.

Rack-and-adhesion motor coach
ABe 4/4 for Rhaetian Railway.

Winter conditions on the Bernina section.

Current used is 11,000-v, 1-phase A.C. of 16⅔ Hz. Type 3 has a 750-hp output, weighs 44 tons and has a 65 km/h maximum speed. It uses 2,200/1,500-v D.C. The Chur–Arosa section is 26-km-long and has a 60 percent maximum gradient. Vehicles are 17,770 mm long, bogie wheel base is 2,550 mm; wheel diameter, 920 mm; 1-hour output, 4 x 275 hp; speed with 60 tons of trailing load, 27 km/h; tare weight, 43.4 tons; and suppliers are BBC, SAAS and Schlieren.

Electric Motor Coaches in Russia

In an official commission's report dated 1920, the 3,000-v D.C. system was recommended as suitable for Russian purposes. Despite this report, the first electrification in the USSR was carried out in 1924 with 1,200/1,500-v D.C. for the 42-km-long line along the Caspian Sea from Baku to Sabuntchi and Surachani. The line was equipped with overhead catenary, and motorcoach trains were employed that consisted of a motor coach with two trailers.

In 1932, the first main line was electrified, all with locomotive-driven trains, and by 1941, 1,865 kilometers were converted, all with 3,000-v D.C. Among the lines electrified were very important ones in the Ural Mountains and in the mineral districts of the Donetz Basin, as well as lines in Siberia. World War II interrupted work, but by 1960 8,700 kilometers were converted, including suburban lines around Moscow, Leningrad, and Baku and the industrial districts of Ural, Donetz, Caucasus, and Siberia.

The Trans-Siberian Railway from Moscow to Irkutsk, 5,194-km-long, was the greatest Russian achievement. As far as Marinsk, 3,000-v D.C. is used, but after that 25,000-v, 1-phase A.C. of 50 cycles is employed, since the USSR, like other countries, experimented with industrial frequency high-tension current.

Knowledge of Russian engineering efforts is difficult to acquire, but details of some powerful and well-designed locomotives built in France, Germany, and Russia have been published.

Already mentioned above is the 1924 electrification of Russian motor coaches. The 1924 vehicles, very similar to American interurbans, were supplied by Elin of Austria and were 4-axled. Their main dimensions were as follows: total length, 18,000 mm; distance between bogie pivots, 12,500 mm; bogie wheel base, 2,400 mm; wheel diameter, 1,050 mm; weight in working order, 38 tons; four motors of 380 hp/1-hour effort with a gear ratio of 1:3.69. Maximum speed was 75 km/h.

For the suburban lines of Moscow, Leningrad, and Kharkov, similar vehicles were ordered from 1930 onwards. These three-coach trains had a center motor coach and two outer driving trailers. They were 19,300 mm long, had a bogie wheel base of 2,400/2,600 mm, and a pivot distance of 14,000 mm. The four motors had a 1-hour output of 816 hp with a gear ratio of 1:3.69. Maximum speed was 85–100 km/h. The vehicles weighed 50 tons.

Similar types were built up until the fifties; the only changes were increased motor output and replacement of wooden bodies by steel ones. Types were built both for 1,500- and 3,000-v D.C. From 1950 onwards, 1,200-hp motor coaches were introduced, which are suitable for maximum speeds of 130–160 km/h and can be used for A.C. and D.C. traction.

Three-coach train for Moscow suburban services of the Russian State Railways.

Two-story motor coach of the Swansea-Mumbles Railway, England, 1929.

The Swansea and Mumbles Railway in England

This line connected the town of Swansea in Wales, an important coal and industrial center, with a nearby spa, Mumbles. It was one of the oldest railway lines not only in Britain but of the world, since it was opened as early as 1809 with horse-drawn traffic that lasted until 1877. Steam traction followed, and in 1928 the line was electrified. It led around Oystermouth Bay and used 650-v D.C. and overhead catenary, after unsuccessful tests with battery-driven vehicles. The standard-gauge line used two-story vehicles of tramway type; they could carry 109 people and were the largest passenger vehicles on British

railways. The railway also used petrol and diesel locomotives and had 13 of the two-floor motor coaches. In 1959, despite considerable local opposition, the line was closed.

Motor Coaches of the Dutch State Railways

After World War I, Dutch railway authorities developed a substantial 1,500-v D.C. electrification program. The original A.C. system was to be changed to D.C. in 1927, with conversion of the lines Amsterdam–Leiden–Hague–Rotterdam and Harlem–Ijmui-

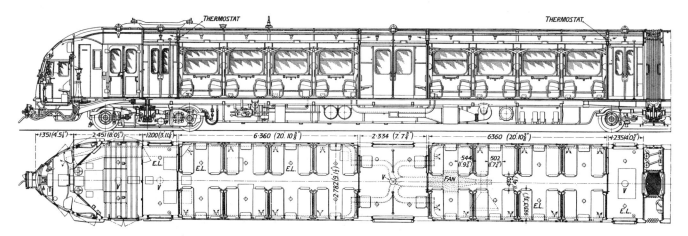

Two-coach train, motorized unit of the N.S., 1934–38.

den. Motorcoach trains with speeds up to 100 km/h were ordered, and trains of up to five units could be run, having a motor coach at each end and trailers in the middle. Coaches equipped with four 200-hp motors weighed 60 tons and trailers, 40 tons. Lines in North Holland were electrified in 1931, followed in 1934 by the Rotterdam–Dordrecht and Rotterdam–Hook van Holland. The first streamlined trains were introduced on these lines to reduce head resistance. Fifty-three twin-motor coaches were ordered, each set having three bogies; 37 three-coach trains

also were ordered. Maximum speed was 120–160 km/h. The motors were nose-suspended and had an output of 300 hp; they were mounted in the outer bogies of the twin-motor coaches.

Only minor developments took place during World War II. The illustrations show the types of vehicles used. The two-coach trains have harmonica connections, while the three-coach units have separate coupled coaches. In the three-coach trains, the outer vehicles are fully motorized with eight motors. The twin-train weighs 79 tons, has 120 seats, and is

Three-coach train set of the N.S., 1934–38.

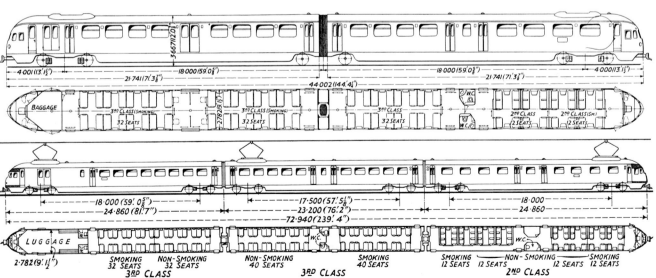

Schematic layout for two- and three-coach train of the N.S., 1934–38.

Motor coach for the 1931 electrification of the Philadelphia, Pa., suburban lines of the Reading Railroad.

Dutch motorcoach train set.

44,102-mm long, while the three-coach train weighs 144 tons, has room for 192 passengers, and is 72,940 mm long. Maximum speed is 125–150 km/h.

The tubular-shaped all-steel bodies were supplied by Werkspoor, Allan, and Beijnes, which paid considerable attention to weight reduction. Wheels have a 900-mm diameter and the 225-hp motors are of the nose-suspended type. The electrical installations were supplied by Metropolitan-Vickers, Heemaf, and Smit.

Since the railways were severely damaged and run down during World War II, extensive reconstructions were ordered after the war ended and motorcoach trains played the leading role. Dutch wagonworks supplied, between 1951 and 1952, 47 four-coach trains and 30 two-coach trains, the electrical installations being supplied by Heemaf of Hengelo. The vehicles can be used in many combinations. For example, the four-coach train can have two outer, fully-motorized motor coaches and two inner trailers.

Main dimensions are as follows: bogie wheel base, 3,000 mm; distance of bogie centers, 18,350 mm; total length of motor coach, 24,950 mm; total length of trailer, 23,530 mm; passenger capacity of four-coach train, 380 (240 seats); passenger capacity of two-coach train, 180 (116 seats); motors per motor coach, four; gear ratio, 22:57; one-hour output per motor, 168 hp (at 1,270 rpm and 675-v); and wheel diameter, 950 mm.

The vehicles have all-welded steel bodies with the characteristic Dutch "nose." Lightweight materials are used extensively. The four-coach trains have a kitchen, the meals being served aircraft-fashion to the passengers at their seats. Similar luggage and mail vehicles were also ordered. Trains can be run in multiple units and all trains are fully air-conditioned.

In 1956/57, similar two- and four-coach trains were ordered, the main difference being the discontinued use of the Jacobs bogie. The driver's cab was strengthened for safety reasons and put in a higher position. The new vehicles are somewhat heavier, with trains weighing 213 tons and 110 tons.

Of major importance were very good running qualities. For this reason, the final bogie design was arrived at after very exhaustive tests. Maximum speed is 165 km/h with a normal traveling speed of 125 km/h. The roof fuse has been replaced by the traditional and more reliable main switch.

The Motor Coaches of the Philadelphia Suburban Lines of the Reading Railroad, U.S.A.

In 1931, this important suburban railway electrified 104 kilometers of line with 251 kilometers of rail length, later extended to 139 and 325 kilometers. A total of 120 motor coaches were ordered with 12,000-v, 1-phase A.C. of 25 cycles. The motor coaches each have four 250-hp motors and are powerful enough to allow quick starting and to cover heavy gradients.

Gear ratio is 1:2.59 and the weight in working order is 63.5 tons; the vehicles can accommodate 86 passengers.

The Motorcoach Trains of the Belgian State Railways

Already by 1903, electrification of the Belgian main line, Brussels–Antwerp, was being considered, but World War I put an end to the plans. It was not until 1935 that the 45-km-long line was electrified with 3,000-v D.C. The work was highly successful and plans were made to connect Brussels electrically with the principal cities of Belgium (Charleroi, Mons, Liège), the so-called Petite Etoile. But again, another world war intervened and it was only from 1945 to 1947 that plans were developed to electrify 1,500 kilometers. For the first section, the electrification of Brussels–Charleroi, 68-km-long, was carried out, followed by the other Belgian main lines.

The difficult terminal stations of the first electrification, Brussels–Antwerp, needed four-coach trains consisting of two outer motor coaches and two inner trailers. Twelve such trains were ordered from Nivelles and Dyle, with Acec and SEM supplying the electrical parts. Main dimensions were as follows: total length of train, 90,360 mm; total weight, fully laden, 274 tons; adhesive weight, 162 tons; capacity, 358 sitting and 55 standing passengers; maximum speed 120 km/h.

Each motor coach has a complete electrical

Motorcoach train for Brussels–Antwerp, SNCB, built by Sécheron.

Motorcoach train of the SNCB, 1955, built by ACEC.

outfit, consisting of two pantographs, main switch, starting resistances, step-controller, reversing switch, motors, and motor-compressor. Two types of control are used: ACEC supplied electropneumatic step-controllers, while SEM supplied air-operated camshaft controllers. The motors are positioned in the frame and power is transmitted by Sécheron spring drive. All trains have multiple-unit control and also a "dead-man" installation.

In the beginning the trains were used for express, non-stop services, and their success encouraged a further order of 16 trailers and another series of trains in the form of eight duplex motor coaches. These appeared in 1939, and had the following main dimensions: total length, 43,040 mm; weight, fully laden, 128 tons; adhesive weight, 76 tons; capacity, 143 seats and 100 standing spaces; maximum speed, 120 km/h.

All vehicles, including the earlier ones, can be interchanged and used in multiple-unit control. Each of the second series of motor coaches had a driving and a running bogie, the first one fully motorized. A novel form of dual-frame bogie was developed by Nivelles: one frame carries the motors and the Sécheron drive and rests on leaf springs; the second frame carries the vehicle body; the motors are controlled electropneumatically.

After World War II, as stated, the complete electrification of the Belgian main lines was decided upon. In addition to locomotives, 25 twin-motor coaches were ordered in 1949/50 for Brussels–Charleroi. Exhaustive tests were undertaken before the orders were placed, although the postwar years presented great problems for railway work. Main data of these trains are as follows: total length, 44,402 mm; total weight, fully laden, 116.5 tons; adhesive weight, 60 tons; capacity, 170 seated and 100 standing passengers; maximum speed, 140 km/h. The motors are of the nose-suspended type and have an output of 260 hp/1-hour. Each bogie of the duplex train has a driving motor, and each of the four Pennsylvania-type bogies thus has one driving and one running axle, reducing the axle-load to 15 tons, while the 1935 vehicles still had an axle-load of 20.25 tons. The new trains have cam-operated contactor gear with servo-motors (type Jeumont-Heidmann).

Attention was paid to weight reduction, and an additional 22 duplex trains were ordered for the further electrification of Brussels–Arlon. Budd stainless steel was used for the body structure and outer skin of the new vehicles, which were ordered from Nivelles, Charleroi, and SEM. The vehicles have the following data: 1-hour output, 736 kw; maximum speed, 120 km/h; weight, 101.5 tons; tare weight, 79.5 tons; total length of train, 45,280 mm. Up to eight vehicles (four trains) can be run in multiple-unit control. Capacity per two-coach train is 171 seats with room for 68 standing passengers.

Again, each train has one motor coach and one trailer; all bogies have one driving and one running axle. The four motors are of the nose-suspended type, have six poles, and have a transmission ratio of 3.73:1.

Motor Coaches of the Austrian Federal Railways

Austria, as one of the pioneering countries of electric traction, used mainly electric locomotives from the beginning. The reason for this was that the Alpine routes with their severe gradients needed such powerful motors that the large units required could not be placed within the limited space available on motor coaches. However, for local traffic, three types of motor coaches were developed between the two world wars. Their main data are in Table 9.

After World War II, it was decided to electrify the main lines of the Oe.B.B. completely, and so three types of motor coaches using novel technical developments were ordered: an express, long-distance motor coach, series 4130; a local traffic motor coach, series 4030; and a luggage motor van, series 4061.

Series ET10 (later 4041) had the main purpose of hauling light trains (such as commuter trains for workmen and school children) when a locomotive

would have been far too powerful for only one or two coaches. In 1929, an economically viable vehicle was developed in this series and supplied by Elin and Krauss in eight units. Seventy-one seats were provided and at the start the motor coach had one driving and one trailing bogie. To reduce axle load, a third axle was built into each bogie. The vehicles were highly successful and, when higher axle loads were allowed, the third axle was removed again.

Series ET11 (later 4042) followed. It is a copy of a diesel-electric vehicle, VT42. It can take one to two trailers and is a typical representative of the design principles of the thirties. Bogies and frames are welded and carry the riveted body. There are two driver's cabs, passenger room (72 seats), and two other rooms for luggage, mail, and parcels.

In 1936, luggage motor van ET30 (now 4060) arrived, which was really a light locomotive with luggage and freight compartments. It can haul three to six vehicles and has two drivers' cabs. As an

Motor coach of the OeBB, series 4041 (formerly ET10).

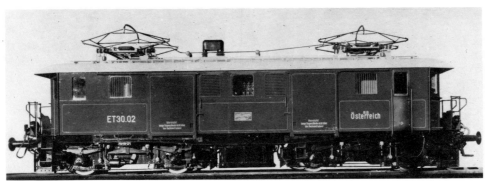

Freight motor coach of the OeBB, series 4042 (formerly ET30).

Table 9
AUSTRIAN FEDERAL RAILWAYS

	New/Old Serial No.: 4041/ET10	New/Old Serial No.: 4042/ET11	New/Old Serial No.: 4060/ET30
Year first built	1929	1936	1936
Wheel arrangement	2–Bo	Bo–2	Bo–Bo
Maximum speed (km/h)	80	100	90
1-hour output (kw) at km/h	516/52.5	460/60.0	800/53.0
Maximum axle load (ton)	20	15.2	16.2
Motors (nose-suspended)	2	2	4
Driving wheel diameter (mm)	1,100	950	950
Wheel base (mm)	16,430	19,160	10,800
Total weight (ton)	73.7	54.6	63.9
Electrical part weight (ton)	22.2	14.6	23.8

example, on the Tauern Line (25‰ gradients) it hauls a 120-ton trailing load at 45–50 km/h.

The first of the newer designs was the express passenger motor coach, series 4130. Originally it was intended for the main east-west (Transalpine) route, Vienna–Innsbruck–Bregenz, but it also was used in international traffic to Zurich and Munich, where two four-coach trains can be run under multiple-unit control. Maximum speed was 130 km/h, gear ratio, 1:3.04, 1-hour output was 1,252 kw, and the 1-hour tractive effort was 5,600 kg with a maximum of 9,500 kg.

The vehicles, built to latest ideas of design and comfort, were supplied by SGP and OeSSW and follow the design layout of series 4030 described below. Instead of the one-sided Sécherôn drive, a two-sided, rubber-ring, spring drive was used. Each train consisted of motor coach, two trailers, and a driving trailer with 96 seats each in first and second class. The high-tension contactor gear has 25 steps with a twin step-switch and servo motor. The motors are of the 8-pole series-connected type. These trains also were used for the highly successful Transalpine express trains that cover the journey from Vienna to

Motor coach series 4042 of the OeBB (formerly ET11).

The new "Transalpin" train, OeBB.

Zurich in 11 hours, a distance of 842 kilometers.

The other series mentioned, Series 4030, was used for commuter services. It was required when the electrification work reached Vienna and its extensive suburban services. Here, the average travel distance is 60 to 120 kilometers, requiring speeds of 120 km/h and a motor output of 1,000 kw/h. The electrical installations were housed in such a manner so as not to interfere with passenger space. A four-coach train was planned, again consisting of motor coach, two trailers, and driving trailer; it could also be used as a two-coach train consisting only of motor coach and driving trailer.

In modified form, 15 trains were ordered for the Vienna Metropolitan Railway (Schnellbahn) in 1960–63. These trains consist of motor coach type 4030.200, trailer 7030.200, and driving trailer 6030.200. Main data of the motor coach are as follows: 1-hour output at 66.5 km/h is 1,000 kw with a tractive effort of 5,360 kg and a maximum tractive effort of 9,300 kg. Maximum speed is 100 km/h; gear ratio, 1:3.41; wheel diameter, 940 mm; bogie pivot distance, 16,250 mm; bogie wheel base, 2,800 mm; total length, 23,190 mm; tare weight, 65 tons. The manufacturer was SGP and the electrical parts were supplied by Elin, AEG, and OeBBC.

As for the technical details of the Vienna Metropolitan Railway coaches, the main frame and bogie frames are made from a welded hollow section, and instead of pivots, supporting pieces are used.

The whole body sits by a crossmember on a cradle; in addition, side bearers are provided. The supporting members are used to transmit power between cradle and body, while guide rods transmit tractive effort from bogie to cradle.

This design enables independent movement of the body against the bogie in vertical, side, and pendular directions. Power transmission is by Sécheron spring drive. The four-coach train has a capacity of 314 seats. All electrical equipment is placed under the body with the transformer in a horizontal position. Only certain control units are inside the coach. The main switch is a BBC air-operated unit; there is no multiple-unit control. The transformer has 14 low-tension steps with two types of control, either step-switches with BBC air-motors or an AEG step-controller with 28 driving steps. Both control installations employ novel ideas about servicing and automation.

The third of the new types, luggage motor van 4061, can haul five trailers with a maximum weight of about 175 tons. The 1-hour output is 1,600 kw at 87.5 km/h; there is a tractive effort of 6,500 kg and a starting effort of 12,000 kg. Other main data are: maximum speed, 125 km/h; gear ratio, 1:2.2059; wheel diameter, 1,040 mm; weight of mechanical part, 39.5 tons; weight of electrical part, 27.5 tons; total weight, 67 tons; total length, 16,170 mm; bogie wheel base, 3,200 mm; distance of bogie centers, 8,100 mm. Suppliers were WLF, Elin, and OeSSW.

Technically, the vehicles follow the same novel ideas as mentioned before, with hollow welded sections for body and bogie frames, extensive use of welding, twin-spring and power transmission effort with cradle and weight transfer system. The same Sécheron drive is used, since it is very suitable for limited space. There are two drivers' cabs, a luggage compartment, and a compartment for the conductor and engine crew. Four driving motors have 400 kw output/1-hour each. Control is by D.C. electropneumatic step-controller. There are two lightweight pantographs (230 kg) and a BBC air-operated main switch. The transformer has 10 low-tension positions with 20 driving and four braking switches. Twelve of these units were supplied in 1958.

Some of the main dimensions of the new vehicles for the Vienna Schnellbahn are found in Table 10.

Originally, four-coach train sets were used, series 4031, a modified form of the suburban type 4030.

By 1962, it was decided to create a special new train, which first went as far as Zurich and then to Basle. The SGP group received instructions to create a six-coach unit for a 150 km/h maximum speed. The train is 16,760 mm long and weighs, in working order, 298.7 tons. It offers 66 first-class and 174 second-class seats. The leading coach is the 4-axled locomotive part, but the last vehicle also has a driver's cab, in addition to luggage space.

Power transmission is carried out by BBC spring drive. For details see pages 110–111. The four motors of the two driving bogies have a 1-hour output of 3,400 hp. All vehicles are permanently linked by central couplers. Coach bodies rest on twin-spring transoms, which in turn sit with long pendulums on the bogie. In addition, there are rubber

Table 10
NEW VEHICLES OF THE SCHNELLBAHN

Type	Series 4030.200	Series 7030.200	Series 6030.200
	Motor coach	Trailer	Driving trailer
Tare weight (ton)	57.1	31.4	31.3
Seats	76	72	56 + luggage
Total length (mm)	23,500	22,990	23,500
Bogie wheel base (mm)	2,700	2,300	2,300
Distance of bogie centers (mm)	16,250	16,250	16,250

A complete four-coach train weighs 119.8 tons empty and 160.3 tons fully laden. It can accommodate 542 passengers. The Schnellbahn vehicles are, of course, very similar to series 4030, but several units can be coupled together; they have automatic doors and lighting equipment.

The New "Transalpin" Train of the Austrian Federal Railways

Among the important intercity connections created by the European railway administrations after World War II was the "Transalpin" from Vienna to Zurich.

springs between bogies and axle boxes, as well as oil-hydraulic dampers to enable smooth running. The train also has an air-conditioned dining car. Main data of the motor coach are as follows:

Wheel arrangement: Bo'-Bo'
Gauge: 1,000 mm
Length: 13,800 mm
Bogie wheel base: 2,650 mm
Seats: 95
Four motors: 1,500-v and 114 kw each
Weight: 22.6 tons
Maximum speed uphill: 1:4–25 km/h
                      downhill: 1:4–15 km/h

The vehicle is built as a self-supporting lightweight type and has two drivers' cabs.

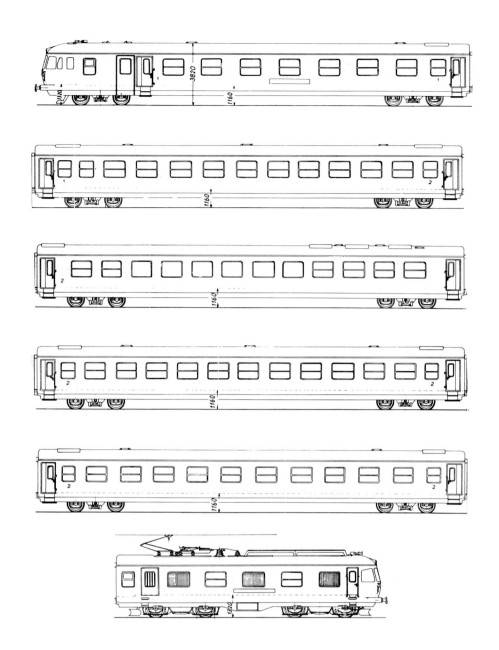

LINE TENSION: 15,000 V.   OUTPUT/4 MOTORS, 70% V MAX - 2500KW

CURRENT: 1-PHASE A.C. 16 2/3 HZ.   TRANSFORMER OUTPUT: 2,730 KVA   MAX. SPEED: 150 KM/H

	DRIVING TRAILER AD 4 ES 6010	TRAILER AB 4 TI 7110.2	DINING CAR BR 4 TI 7310	TRAILER B 4 TI 7110.1	TRAILER D 4 ET 4010
WEIGHT, TARE:	38.1 T	38.6 T	42.9 T	38.8 T	37.1 T
WEIGHT, LADEN:	44.4 T	46.6 T	45.3 T	45.5 T	45.1 T
SEATS:	42 (1st CLASS)	60 (1 & 2nd CLASS)	9 + 34 DINER	66-2nd CLASS	60 2nd CLASS

	DRIVING MOTOR COACH D4 ET 4010	TOTAL 6-COACH TRAIN
WEIGHT, TARE:	68.8 T	264.3 T
WEIGHT, LADEN	69.8 T	298.7 T
SEATS:	---	237 (66 1st CLASS & 171 2nd CLASS)

CARRIAGE:	1	2	3	4	5
SEATS:	42	---	DINER & BAR	42	42
TARE WEIGHT:	40T	102T	40T	37T	40T

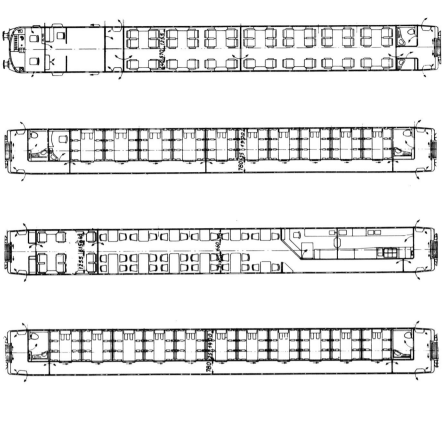

6-COACH MOTORCOACH TRAIN
"TRANSALPIN"
237 SEATS (66-1st CLASS & 171 2nd CLASS)
MAX. SPEED: 150KM/H

DRIVING TRAILER AD 4 ES.6010.01-03	TRAILER AB4TI 7110.201-203
DINING CAR BB TI 7310.01-03	TRAILER B4TI 7110.101-103
TRAILER B 4TI 7010.101-103	MOTOR-COACH 4010.01-03

SMOKING AND NON-SMOKING SECTIONS AVAILABLE
ON ALL COACHES

Suburban motorcoach train of the LMS Railway, England, for its London suburban traffic, 1930.

The Electrification of the London Suburban Lines of the LMS Railway, England

This important electrification took place between 1914 and 1927 and comprised the following three sections: the former L & N.W. R. suburban sections (68 line and 150 rail kilometers); the Whitechapel and Bow lines of the LMS and the Metropolitan and District Railway; and the 7-kilometer line (23-kilometer rail) until Barking (Midland section).

Electrical services began in 1914 with the line Willesden Junction–Earls Court–Broad Street to Hampstead Heath, Kew Bridge, and Richmond. In 1917, Watford Junction was reached, and in 1922 followed Euston–Camden Town, Watford–Croxley Green, and finally the line to Rickmansworth in 1927.

Current used is 600–630-v D.C. supplied through third and fourth rail. The trains ordered from Metropolitan-Vickers were three-coach units, consisting of motor coach, trailer, and driving trailer. All fully-motorized coaches have four units of 280-hp 1-hour effort. The driving vehicles have a driver's cab, engine and luggage room, and a passenger compartment.

Although very heavy by today's design standards, the vehicles are still in use and are known for their reliability and smooth-riding qualities. In 1927, an additional order was placed for 28 motor coaches, 24 trailers, and 23 driving trailers.

The Electrification of the Eastern Suburban Lines of London (Liverpool Street–Shenfield), England

London's Liverpool Street station serves the extensive suburban areas east of the city. Lines go through densely populated areas and ultimately reach Shenfield, a distance of 37 kilometers. The entire line is four-tracked.

In 1936, the former LNER decided to electrify the line with 1,500-v D.C. and overhead catenary. The work was interrupted by World War II and recommenced in 1946; electric services started in 1949. In all, 138 kilometers were electrified. Initially, 92 three-coach trains were ordered, the suppliers being Metropolitan-Cammell, Birmingham Carriage and Wagon, and English Electric. Vehicles were designed especially for very dense commuter services. In the one-hour traffic period from 5 to 6 p.m., for example, 16 express trains are operated.

The vehicles have the following main dimensions: total length of three-coach train, 54,116 mm; length of motor coach, 18,400 mm; tare weight of train, 104.7 tons; tare weight of motor coach, 50.8 tons; motor bogie wheel base, 2,400 mm; seating capacity, 176 with room for 220 standing passengers; wheel diameter, 1,093 mm; gear ratio, 71/17; maximum tractive effort, 9,000 kg; 1-hour tractive effort at 52 km/h, 4,500 kg; and maximum speed, 112 km/h.

Each train consists of a motor coach, trailer, and

Nine-coach train for the LNER electrification of Liverpool Street Station–London–Shenfield, England, 1,500-v D.C.

Twin-set motorcoach train for the Manchester–Sheffield line across the Pennines, 1,500-v D.C., LNER, England.

driving trailer. The vehicles are of welded all-steel construction in which the frame is load-bearing. Each motor coach is fully motorized with four nose-suspended units. These are of the 4-pole series-connected type of 210 hp/1-hour output. Each train has only one pantograph and main switch; there are two motor-circuits of two motors each that are permanently series-connected. Control is by electro-pneumatic contactor gear with 17 steps. Multiple-unit control is available to run up to three trains together.

The Electrification of the Manchester–Sheffield Line, England

This important line across the Pennines mainly uses locomotives. For the suburban sections of Manchester, three-coach trains were ordered, supplied by General Electric, Metropolitan-Cammell, and Birmingham Carriage and Wagon Company.

On the line across the Pennines, eight three-coach trains were supplied, consisting of motor coach, trailer, and driving trailer, whereby two trains

Table 11
MANCHESTER–SHEFFIELD LINE

	Motor Coach	Trailer	Driving Trailer
Length (mm)	18,400	15,920	15,650
Bogie wheelbase (mm)	2,600	2,440	2,440
Distance of bogie pivots (mm)	12,375	11,590	11,590
Tare weight (tons)	50.6	26.4	27.4
Maximum speed (km/h)	112	112	112

could be run in multiple-unit control. There is only one pantograph, one roof main switch, and four nose-suspended motors, which are coupled in pairs in series-connection and have a 1-hour output of 185 hp. They have electropneumatic contactor gear with 17 steps. Main data are in Table 11.

The Experimental Motor Coaches for Industrial Frequency (50 Hertz) of the SNCF & of the DB

For its La Rôche-sur-Foron–Aix-les-Bains experimental line with 50 Hz traction, the SNCF in 1950 not only ordered test locomotives, but also two motor coaches that were the first attempt to apply 50-cycle traction to motorcoach trains. One of these vehicles was originally in possession of the DR and ran under 15,000-v, 1-phase A.C. of the 16⅔ Hz. The SNCF rebuilt it for 20,000-v 50-cycles using 50-cycle direct-commutator motors. The other electrical installations were taken over unaltered.

One bogie of each coach half is motorized with two motors, while the other bogie is a running one. The motors have a 1-hour output of 480 hp, which is 1,920 hp for the twin-coach. Each half weighs 48 tons and takes 61 passengers. The reason for this modest number is that a special room was created to hold the electrical test installations. There are also two drivers' cabs.

In addition, a motorcoach train, Z.9051 and ZS.19051, was ordered consisting of a motor coach and driving trailer. The vehicles came from the Paris–Etampes route, and were reconstructed in the

1,730-hp motorcoach train for suburban traffic, SNCF, series Z.9051 and ZS.19051 for 50-cycle traction, MFO.

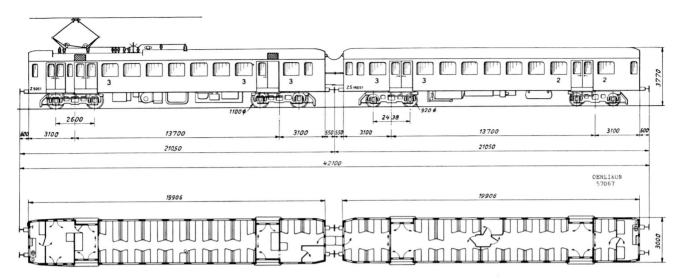

Schematic layout of motorcoach train series Z.9051 and ZS.19051.

workshops at Oullins near Lyons. With 50-Hz traction, the vehicle has four motors with 1-hour output of 1,730 hp. The two-coach train weighs 126 tons, 77 tons being the weight of the motor coach.

Tests were conducted to prove whether 50-Hz motor coaches were equal to the successful and proven D.C. suburban vehicles that had shown their reliability in many years of regular commuter services. Under 1,500-v D.C., the vehicle had four nose-suspended motors of 247 hp/1-hour with a total weight of 64 tons, the electrical installation weighing 19.5 tons. Under 50-Hz traction, both output and weight were increased due to the ventilating system for the 50-Hz motors and because of the heaviest piece of equipment, the transformer, which was placed in the center of the motor coach.

Since speeds of 120 km/h or more were expected, the nose suspension was changed to an Oerlikon drive. The new motors weighed 1,600 kg and had an output of 445 hp at 251-v and 1670A, whereby the tractive effort was 8,160 kg at 51.7 km/h. Maximum speed was 80 km/h. Control was by electromechanical step switches.

One train set began work in 1951 and after 18 months had run over 160,000 kilometers without any special difficulties. It was thus proved from the start that 50-cycle traction was suitable for intensive suburban services.

In 1948, the former South-West German Railway Administration (SWDE) placed an order to rebuild a war-damaged motor coach into a 50-Hz twin-motor coach using 50-cycle commutator motors, similar to the successful test locomotives of the Black Forest or Hoellenthal Railway. The electrical installations were supplied by SSW (as before) and Rastatt Waggonworks carried out the rebuilding.

The motorcoach unit was numbered ET255.01 and had two halves, each with a driver's cab and one running and one motorized bogie. Main data were as follows: wheel arrangement Bo'2' + 2'Bo'; total weight, 130 tons; adhesive weight, 63.6 tons; axle load, 15.9 tons; driving wheel diameter, 1,050 mm; gear ratio, 69:14; 1-hour tractive effort at 67.5 km/h was 8,400 kg; and maximum speed was 90 km/h.

To satisfy the difficult conditions on the Hoellenthal line, especially the heavy gradients of 55%oo, the entire electrical installation had to be redeveloped, especially since high-powered motors were required. Their size—as well as the ventilating installations, transformers, and switchgear—made accommodation in a motor coach difficult.

Control was carried out by 11-step step-switch control. From this control, the current went to a current-divider and then to the motors before returning to the transformer. The most interesting components were the 50-Hz commutator motors, which were very different from the 16⅔-cycle motors because they had an increased number of poles, higher amperages, and lower voltages. Each driving axle was driven by two motors, coupled permanently in series. The 1-hour output per twin motor was 385 kw at 1,735 rpm, 1,950 A, 243-v and a cos ϕ of

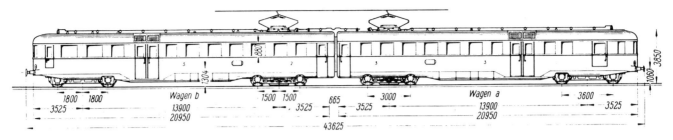

Rebuilt twin motorcoach set, series ET255.01 of the DB.

0.96. This compares with the motors of the Hoellenthal test locomotive as follows: 257 kw, 1,890 rpm, 1,370 A, 243-v, cos ϕ = 0.95.

Output consequently was almost 50 percent higher at the same weight, demonstrating the progress made in 20 years in the design of 50-cycle motors. Motor weight was about the same at 2.5 tons and they were again of the nose-suspended type. In addition, a magnetic railbrake was introduced.

Motorcoach Trains for India

Originally, three railway companies in British India had electrified lines that primarily were suburban sections using 1,500-v D.C. The three lines were the 1,676 mm-gauge Great Indian Peninsula Railway (GIP), the 1,676 mm-gauge Bombay, Baroda & Central Indian Railway (BB & CI Railway), and the 1,000 mm-gauge South Indian Railway (SI Railway).

The GIP Railway electrified its first line at Bombay in 1925 and reached Kalyan, 53 kilometers distant, in 1929 with four rails throughout. Later the electric system was extended to Poona and Igatpuri using mostly locomotives. The BB and CI Railway electrified its suburban sections in Bombay in 1928, and the SI Railway operated the electric line Madras–Tambaram, 31-km-long, from 1931.

For the electrification of the SI Railway and the Madras suburban lines, British firms in 1931 supplied 24 three-coach trains with Jacobs bogies in which the center vehicle was the motor coach with 480-hp motors and the two outer vehicles were driving trailers. The vehicles can be used in multiple-unit control as three-, six- and nine-coach trains. Total length of the three-coach train is 46,060 mm, and bogie wheel base is 2,590 mm. A train weighs 79 tons empty and offers 194 seats. Maximum speed

Motorcoach for the Great Indian Peninsula Railway, now Indian State Railways.

Motorcoach train for India, built by Breda, Italy.

Postwar motorcoach train for India, built by Breda, Italy.

is 90 km/h. Seven similar trains later were ordered from English Electric and Gloucester Carriage and Wagon Company.

When railways were nationalized in India, plans for extensions of electric traction were developed. In 1951, several British firms supplied the Indian State Railways with seven four-coach trains, each consisting of two outer motor coaches and two inner trailers. The vehicles were intended for Calcutta suburban services.

Each of the vehicles has six sliding double doors that can be operated by hand or by electricity. The vehicles are built as self-supporting units using lightweight materials extensively, including plastic. The roof and side walls are completely insulated—an essential feature since the trains have to work in high tropical temperatures (more than 40°C or 104°F). The insulation consists of a five-layer isoflex fixed with wiremesh. Lighting is by fluorescent tubes.

The motors are 4-pole series-connected units, four per motor coach and with 175-hp 1-hour output at 700-v. Transmission gear is 61:19 with 903 mm-diameter driving wheels. The electrical installations are contained in special high-tension chambers. Tare weight of the motor coach is 52 tons and of the trailer, 31 tons. Current is 1,400-v D.C.; gauge, 1,676 mm; catenary supply; and maximum speed, 112 km/h. There are 415 seats per four-coach train.

In addition, several Swiss firms (SIG, SWS, BBC, and MFO) supplied 16 trains; so did the German firms of AEG and MAN. These trains consisted of a central motor coach and two driving trailers. The vehicles are similar to the ones described above and have remote-controlled electro-pneumatic contactor gear with automatic starting devices and multiple-unit control.

Triplex motor coaches, wheel arrangement 2'1'+B'1'+1'2', built by AEG for the DR.

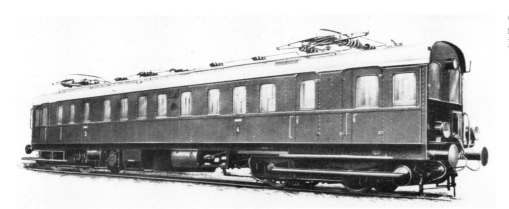

(1A)2' motor coach of the DR for the suburban traffic of Magdeburg, DR, SSW.

Motor Coaches and Motorcoach Trains of the DR and DB, Germany

Until the arrival of the automobile as a serious competitor for rail traffic, the motor coach played only a minor role in Germany. It was in the thirties, as bigger electrification schemes were carried out in and around major metropolitan areas, that more substantial motorcoach services were introduced, both for intercity and suburban transport. The beginnings of the electric motor coach and the pioneering accomplishments are described beginning on page 1.

In 1920, the AEG firm supplied triplex-motor coaches for the Silesian electrification scheme. Actually, the coaches consisted of a middle unit in the form of a small locomotive, from which power was transmitted from motor to wheels by coupling rods. The motorcoach train had the wheel arrangement 2'1'+B'1'+1'2', which means that each component vehicle had three axles with the driving part in the center. The complete train was 42,520 mm long, had 114 seats, and room for 40 standees. It was planned

for the heavily graded suburban services in Silesia. Weight in working order was 98.5 tons and, in the 1-hour tractive effort, was 2 x 310 hp with 1:3.74 transmission ratio.

Another vehicle was supplied by SSW in two units with the (1A)'-2' wheel arrangement and with 1,200 mm driving wheels. It was designed for the Magdeburg–Rothensee line, and accommodated 52 sitting and 65 standing passengers. It was 21,900 mm long and weighed 59 tons in working order. The two motors had a 1-hour output of 330 hp each, gear ratio was 1:3.23, and 80 km/h was the maximum speed.

For the Silesian lines, a (1'A') (A'1') motor coach was supplied in 1926 with a maximum speed of 65 km/h. It was 21,900 mm long, carried 100 passengers, and weighed 68.5 tons. It had two 340-hp motors (1-hour output) with a gear ratio of 1:4.17.

For the important electrification of Halle–Leipzig, SSW supplied (1'A') (A'1') motor coaches in 1927 for express services. They were 22,900 mm long, had 66 seats, and maximum speed was 100

(1A) (A1) motor coach of the DR, built in 1926 by SSW for the Silesian lines.

(1A) (A1) express motor coach of the DR, built in 1927 by SSW for Halle–Leipzig.

Bo'-2' motor coach of the DR for its Bavarian network, built by BBC-Mannheim.

km/h. Weight in working order was 65.7 tons, and the two motors had a 1-hour output of 340 hp with a gear ratio of 1:3.285.

In 1935, an interesting design appeared—the electric "panoramic view" motor coach ET91. It was of steel construction with a glass roof, low windows, and air-smoothed ends. The vehicle thus permitted excellent observation of the surrounding countryside and was specially intended for tourist traffic in Bavaria and Wurtemberg; it also was used for trips to Switzerland and Austria.

The vehicles have two compartments of 36 seats each, air conditioning, and air heating. They were 20,080 mm long and had two bogies, one of which was fully motorized with two 265-hp (per 1 hour) motors. Bogie wheelbase was 3,600 mm and wheel diameter was 950 mm, with a gear ratio of 1:3.35. The electrical installation was placed in the motor bogie and frame. Total weight was 49 tons. Two vehicles were supplied by Fuchs and AEG. They were a considerable success and were found very attractive by the traveling public.

A three-section motorcoach train was supplied in 1937 by Linke-Hoffmann. The train consisted of two end-motor coaches and a center vehicle, making the total train 23,050/22,750 mm long. The driving bogie had a wheel base of 3,600 mm and running bogies of 3,000 mm, wheel diameter was 970 mm, and weights in working order were 48.6 + 46.4 + 48.6 tons. Each vehicle had a driving and a running bogie. There were 188 seats. Since the motor bogies had two motors each, the complete train had six nose-suspended motors of 370 hp/1-hour output. Maximum speed was 120 km/h.

Motor coach of the DR, built in 1934–35 for the Stuttgart suburban lines.

Postwar suburban motor coach series ET56 for the DR.

Motor coach of DR, series ET91, with glass roof for tourist services.

Motorcoach Trains of the DB after World War II, Germany

At the beginning of the 1950s, the DB developed several motorcoach trains for its suburban services to be used on 16⅔-cycle lines with a maximum speed of 90 km/h. Each motorcoach train consists of three close-coupled components with the outer parts motorized. In all, there are four motors with a 1-hour output of 225 kw each at 77 km/h, which are housed in the outer bogies of the motorcoach parts and are nose-suspended. The train has two pantographs, a BBC air-operated main switch, and a transformer that is fixed under the coach frame.

The electrical installation follows established practices, but the coach part is built using novel ideas. The whole of the body and underframe form a self-supporting tube. The floor part is hollow and contains the entire electrical installation and brake systems; the under-floor part is force-ventilated.

All components subject to regular inspection or overhaul are accessible from the outside through folding doors and can be withdrawn, since they are contained in drawer-like units. Body and bogies are built in all-welded construction and the body rests over cross-members and side-pieces on double leaf-springs and dampers so that the pivot is used for traction purposes only.

The complete train is 80,000 mm long and weighs only 116 tons. It carries 240 first-class passengers and 238 in second class, so that, including standing room, 480 passengers are accommodated; there is also a luggage compartment. The trains were supplied in 1952 by Esslingen, Fuchs & Rathgeber, while the electrical installations were furnished by AEG, BBC, and SSW.

The Motorcoach Train ET30 for the Ruhr Express Services, Germany

With the success of electrified rail services before and after the war in the areas of Munich, Nuremberg, and Stuttgart, as well as in Silesia, it was decided in 1957 to introduce motorcoach traffic in the Ruhr district and connect the major centers of the Rhenish–Westphalian area. Such services needed high speeds, ample seating, and comfort to lure travelers back from the road to the railway.

The vehicles were to have traveling speeds up to 120 km/h and accelerating speeds of 0.7 m/sec^2. The trains were to provide ample room for 400 to 1,200 passengers.

To meet these demands, the three-coach ET30 unit was developed, consisting of two motor coaches and a center trailer, all close-coupled. Capacity is 441 passengers. AEG and BBC developed a special motor with a 1-hour output of 660 kw, the outer bogies of the two motor coaches being motorized. The transformer has a 26-step AEG low-tension contactor gear. The electrical installations, including the transformer, are housed in the motor bogies and under the body floor.

Comfort of the passengers and wide view-windows were considered essential. The control gear is semi-automatic. Other main data are as follows: maximum speed, 120 km/h; 30 seats in first class and 192 in second class; standing room, 215; total length of three-coach train, 80,360 mm; wheel arrangement, Bo'2 + 2'2' + 2'Bo'; wheel base of motor bogie, 3,600 mm; running bogie, 2,500 mm; wheel diameters, driving, 1,100 mm, running, 900 mm; weight, fully laden, 181.6 tons; axle load, 20.5 tons, maximum.

The S-Bahn Motor Coaches, Series ET 27, Germany

From 1961 to 1964, more vehicles were developed especially for the dense traffic conditions of fast suburban services with short station distances (about 2.5 kilometers) and difficult platform positions. The trains were laid out for maximum speeds of 120 km/h.

The three-coach train had the wheel arrangement Bo'Bo' + 2'2' + Bo'Bo'. The center section contained no electrical parts so that two coach trains (without the center trailer) could be formed. The floor was only 900 mm above railhead, which meant that the outer motor diameter could not be larger than 600 mm. The construction and positioning of the main transformer also presented considerable problems.

The motors were single-phase, since those for mixed currents continued to cause difficulties. The motors had a constant output of 150 kw at 2,260 rpm. The three-coach trains had 185 seats and offered 265 to 398 passengers seating and standing room. The vehicles were supplied by AEG, BBC Mannheim, and Wegmann. The first five trains proved themselves with good running qualities and soundproofing.

Main data were as follows: There were eight nose-suspended motors of 1,200 kw constant output and gearing of 4.33:1. The tare weight was 134 tons and the total length was 73,730 mm. Distance of bogie pivots was 16,650 mm for the motor coach and 15,650 mm for the trailer. Bogie wheel base was 2,500 mm and wheel diameter, 900 mm.

Italian Motor Coaches and Motorcoach Trains

The Italian State Railways have used motor coaches since 1936, all on D.C. lines. The ETR200 series, built in 1936, consists of a three-coach train with a total length of 62,000 mm. Fifteen close-coupled trains were ordered with a 1-hour output of 1,140 kw/h. There were six motors, maximum speed was 160 km/h, and total weight was 117 tons. These trains were rebuilt in 1960 as four-coach units.

Typical of Italian railways are the 35 two-coach trains of 1950 designed for 3,000-v D.C., which

Motorcoach train of the Italian State Railways for 3,000-v D.C. and 3,400-v, 3-phase A.C. built by CGE, Milan.

3,000-v D.C. motorcoach train for Italy.

consist of motor coach ALe 840 and driving trailer RLe 840. Motor coaches weigh 57 tons; there are 84 seats. The four 1,500-v motors have a 1-hour output of 1,150 hp for the four units. Maximum speed is 150 km/h. Later, another 33 units were ordered. Each coach is 28,000 mm long, has a bogie wheel base of 3,000 mm, and a pivot distance of 20,000 mm. Series ALe 660, built in 1955 with first-class compartments, is of identical design.

The Electric Express Motorcoach Trains ETR 300 and ETR 250, Italy

In 1954, the Italian State Railways ordered three luxuriously equipped train sets, series ETR 300, named "Settebello." They were to comprise the latest ideas in passenger comfort and appeal. The train consists of seven vehicles—four passenger coaches, one dining car, one kitchen car, and one luggage and service van. The complete train is 165,500 mm long, has a tare weight of 324 tons, and has 20 axles. There are drivers' cabs at both ends. The wheel arrangement is Bo'2'Bo' + Bo'2'2'Bo' + Bo'2'Bo'.

Vehicles have the following main dimensions: passenger vehicles 1 and 7, 24,500 mm long; restaurant and luggage vehicle and passenger vehicles 2, 3, 5, and 6, 24,125 mm long; and kitchen car (No. 4), 20,000 mm long.

The running bogies are of the Jacobs type, have a 3,000 mm wheel base, and a 1,040 mm wheel diameter (No's. 2, 5, 6 and 9); the six driving bogies are numbered 1, 3, 4, 7, 8, and 10; they have the same wheel base and wheel diameter. The train has 238 seats, and has 12 motors with a 1-hour output of 190 kw each (the motors can be connected in series, series-parallel, and parallel). Transmission gear ratio is 33:53, whereby the tractive forces are transmitted by a Fanelli rubber-ring drive; maximum speed is 180 km/h.

In 1960, four similar series ETR 250 four-coach trains were purchased. The trains are 97,250 mm long and have six motors with 1-hour output of 250 kw each. Maximum speed also is 180 km/h. The complete train weighs 181 tons and, again, very modern design ideas were used. Here, as well as in the ETR 300, Jacob's bogies were used as the center bogies of the two train-halves. In the ETR 250, three bogies are of the running type and three are motorized. Again, the motors are placed next to the axle, and power-transmission is carried out by the Fanelli rubber-ring drive. The vehicles of both trains were supplied by the firm of Breda.

In 1957, the Italian Railways ordered an unusual type of motorcoach train that was to run both under 3,000-v D.C. and 3,700-v, 3-phase A.C. The three-car train, consisting of a normal D.C. motor coach (all 840, ALe 840, or ALe 660, as described above), is coupled with a rebuilt trailer, series Le 840, carrying

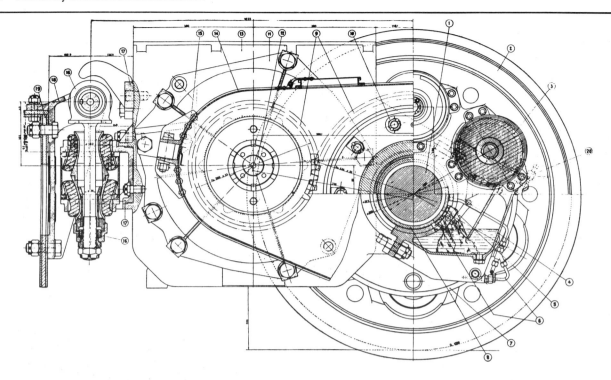

Sectional view (elevation) of Fanelli individual axle drive for motorcoach train ETR200.

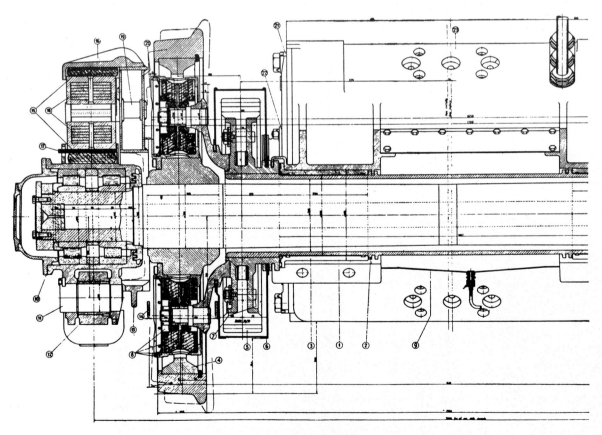

Cross section

Express motorcoach train ETR 300, the Italian "Settebello."

two 3-phase pantographs and the rectifier installation. The third vehicle is a normal driving trailer, Le 800.

To simplify operation as much as possible, it was specified that the trailer was to be reconstructed in such a manner that it could be added to any normal D.C. two-coach train. That meant that the whole converter installation had to be in (or under) one vehicle. After various innovative ideas of rectification were investigated (Selenium, Germanium), it was decided to use a single-anode mercury-arc rectifier (excitron) with an air-cooled transformer. The whole development was a major pioneering effort because it was the first attempt to use D.C. 3-phase A.C. vehicles as motor coaches. The work was carried out by General Electric/Milan, Brown Boveri, and the workshops of the Italian State Railways.

In 1958, another express motor coach, series ALe 540 with trailer Le 760, appeared, supplied by

Ocren of Naples. Furthermore, two types of motorcoach trains were developed in the early sixties, one for intercity transport and one for express suburban services. The first one to appear, series ALe 601, was for speeds up to 160 km/h and first class only. The vehicles have 60 seats and full air-conditioning; each coach is 27,400 mm long with a pivot-distance of 18,200 mm. There are four 250-hp motors. The trailer is of the Le 840 or Le 601 type. The Le 480 is a luxury dining car.

The second type of train ordered, series ALe 803, is, as already mentioned, designed for fast suburban services. The train has three vehicles, the motor coach has the wheel arrangement Bo'Bo', and there is a center trailer and a driving end trailer. With a maximum speed of 130 km/h, the train has 4 x 250 kw/1-hour motors (at 65 km/h). These vehicles made it possible to increase traveling speeds between 1953 and 1960 by about 30 km/h.

"Variable-Inclination"
motorcoach train of the F.S.

The Variable-Inclination Electric Motorcoach Train for the F.S., Italy

The F.S. ordered the variable-inclination electric motor coach as a test unit from Messrs. Fiat to try to ascertain its effects on high-speed trains running on electrified multicurve main lines. Other participants in the work were Marelli and Ansaldo; a similar train was ordered by Renfe.

The basic idea is to use speeds up to 250 km/h (155 mph) on curving main lines, thus avoiding costly rebuilding. The "controlled inclination" device is thus to be used to limit centrifugal acceleration in bends to 0.8 m/s². As an example, on a 450 m curve, the permitted maximum speed is 100 km/h. A speed of 135 km/h would still be safe but not permitted, as it would annoy passengers by giving an acceleration of 2.16 m/S². With controlled inclination, however, the curve can be taken at considerably higher speeds in perfect comfort. To achieve maximum speed, a lightweight train is needed to reduce both train mass and track stress.

A triple braking system was introduced, namely pneumatic disc brakes, a rheostat brake, and electromagnet rail brake-shoes. The four-car train has cabs at both ends and may be varied to work as two-, six-, eight-, or ten-coach units. Motors are distributed throughout the train to avoid excessive weight concentrations. Each vehicle has two bogies carrying two motors that drive one axle of each bogie.

There is vertical and transverse suspension to allow only a certain amount of centrifugal movement before the compensating device comes into action. This inward-inclination is in the form of a hydraulic

control between coach and bogies. The whole coach forms a strengthened tubular structure. The trains are fully air-conditioned and soundproofed. Each bogie is made up of an articulated chassis and is connected to the axle-boxes by springs and rubber elements to ensure lateral stability. The body rests on a swinging cross-member that in turn rests on screw spring units.

Traction and braking efforts are transmitted by the chassis, bogies, and cross-members by means of a precompressed rubber device. The entire system is controlled by hydraulic servo-assisted sensors. The pantograph is supported on a special frame that rests on the swinging cross-member and is independent of body movements.

The motors, fitted to the body, transmit power by universal shafts and axles with cone-shaped torque. Each coach thus has four 1,500-v traction motors, coupled in series.

The special inclination of the body is achieved hydraulically by two cylinders that act between the swinging member and two anchorages in the framework. The flow in the cylinders is regulated from zero to maximum rotation velocity through valves. The control of the inclination has to be not only correct but also instant, acting only in the curve and not before entering it. At 180 km/h, this allows only two seconds for action.

An accelerometer is used, but is suitably filtered and adjusted to act correctly. This compensation is carried out as follows: a gyroscope is placed on the bogie and signals the required action; it avoids action through normal track irregularities and only acts when the super-elevation exceeds 10 mm; the delay

"Variable-Inclination" motor coach driver's cab with control desk.

of transmitting the signal is only one-tenth of a second. The gyroscope signal activates a trapezoidal stress device from zero to maximum, when it stays constant until the gyroscope stops.

Extensive tests have been undertaken since 1972 on the Florence–Rome main line at speeds of 126 km/h.

Newer Vehicles for the Stockholm Suburban Lines, Sweden

In 1960, the Swedish State Railways ordered for the ever-increasing suburban traffic several motor coach trains, all of three-coach design, that also could be run in multiple-unit control as nine- and twelve-coach trains. The trains are laid out for a maximum speed of 100 km/h. They have disc brakes for the trailer wheels and combined disc and rheostatic brakes for the motor coaches. Each three-coach unit has ample rush-hour room for 310 sitting and 150 standing passengers.

Main dimensions are as follows: wheel diameter, 966 mm; bogie wheel base, (trailer) 2,400 mm, (motor coach) 2,600 mm; distance of pivots, 18,000 mm; lengths, 24,060/23,400 mm; tare weights, 39 and 39.6 tons (trailers) and 65.4 tons (motor coach); total length of three-coach train, 74,360 mm; total weight, 144 tons; motors, 4 x 375 hp equaling 1,500 hp per train; and gear ratio, 80:19. The electrical part was supplied by ASEA.

In 1967, total reorganization of the Stockholm transport system resulted in an order of 102 series XI two-coach trains that contained a number of novel technical features. Starting acceleration was increased to 0.6 m/sec^2 and maximum speed to 120 km/h. Five of these two-coach trains can be coupled together. There are 300 seats per two-coach train, or 1,500 per ten-coach train. Again, ASEA supplied the electrical installations, while the vehicles were delivered by ASJ, Linköping, Kalmar, and Oy Tampella.

1,360 hp, LITT.XOA5 three-coach train set for Sweden.

Motorcoach set for Stockholm suburban services, Swedish State Railways.

Drawer with six thyristors and main switch for 15 kv 630A, 16⅔ Hz 250-MVA output.

Drawer with six thyristors and main switch for 15 kv 630A, 16⅔ Hz 250-MVA output.

Partially sectioned pressure contact thyristor, built by ASEA.

Main dimensions per two-coach train are as follows: 1-hour output of the four motors, 1,525 hp; total length, 49,550 mm; distance of bogie centers, 18,200 mm; bogie wheel base, 2,200/2,400 mm; wheel diameter, 920 mm; tare weights for motor coach, 48.1 tons, and for driving trailer, 29.3 tons; total per two-coach train, 77.4 tons.

Quick and easy acceleration and braking characteristics were considered most important. In addition, maintenance work was to be as minimal as possible. The innovations thus developed were considered the latest in rail vehicle design. The bogies have disc brakes and the inner bogie of the driving trailer also has a magnetic rail brake. The bogies are practically free of maintenance requirements because there are no wearing parts between bogies and underframe.

There are four motors, all fed from one rectifier. To increase its efficiency, the transformer is divided into three windings, each of which supplies bridge-connected diodes and thyristors. The transformer is oil-cooled and has a characteristic of 15,000-v/3 x 365, 1,000 and 230-v. The three-part rectifier is air-cooled, and the semi-conductors are contained in drawer-like boxes for easy maintenance. The diode units have five diodes each, and the thyristor drawer contains the respective thyristor types for field and anchor control.

Very interesting is the control and regulation of the motors. After the voltage (i.e., speed) and tractive effort are selected, the following sequence of events is brought automatically into action: the bridge allows the driving motors to receive first one-third of their full tension. To increase voltage and speed further, the first bridge is reduced and the second one is opened. Then the first bridge is reopened and the motors receive two-thirds of their full tension. In the same way, the third bridge is brought into action until the motors receive their full voltage.

Lightweight Motor Coaches and Motorcoach Trains in Sweden

Sweden is not only thinly populated, but distances between towns are considerable; in addition, motor traffic is a heavy rail competitor. Under these circumstances, motorcoach traffic (whether diesel or electric) seems to provide an answer to the survival of minor or branch lines, especially if such traffic is to be economically viable.

Swedish vehicles have one-man control and are so simple to operate that they do not need fully qualified engine drivers. Because the country has ample water power, electrifications started early, thus beginning the need for simple, lightweight motor coaches. The firm of H. Carlsson developed a type of electric rail bus for narrow-gauge lines, and Messrs. ASJ did the same for standard-gauge lines.

Today, there are several hundred of these vehicles in use. An example of these vehicles is series YB.oab, purchased by the Swedish State Railways in 1955/56 in 30 units from ASEA and ASJ. The train actually is a diesel railbus in which the diesel engine has been replaced by an electric motor. The motor is fixed longitudinally under the body as is the transformer, which extends partly into the coach itself. The vehicle has a seven-step contactor gear and no main switch, only fuses. The motor has a 1-hour output of 230 hp and drives the axles by a Cardan shaft. Capacity is 55 passengers.

Express Motorcoach Trains for Stockholm–Göteborg, Sweden

The 456-km-long Stockholm–Göteborg line is the main traffic artery of Sweden. Electrification of steam locomotives took place in 1928 and reduced traveling time from nine to six hours. Eventually, express motorcoach trains were ordered to reduce the run to 4¾ hours.

Initial tests were made with an existing vehicle

15,000-v, 1-phase A.C. 16⅔ Hz railbus, series YBoa7 for Sweden.

Swedish lightweight motor coach and trailer.

(LITT.Xoa7) from the suburban services. This 1,200-hp-output vehicle reached 120 km/h without difficulty with a maximum axle-load of only 13.5 tons.

The trains finally ordered were of the three-coach type, series Xoa5. Starting work in 1948, the trains have two driving end-trailers, one for second and another for third class. The inner bogies of these vehicles are motorized, while the high-tension installation is housed in a special compartment in the center coach. Output is 4 x 340 hp = 1,360 hp/1-hour. Weight in working order is 154 tons.

The trains were to have a traveling speed of 100 km/h and a maximum speed of 156 km/h going uphill (10‰ gradients) or downhill. The very successful trains received such names as Göteborger and ran through the 456-kilometer distance in 4 hours and 50 minutes, which included 312 kilometers without stop. Each train returns on the same day after a daily round-trip run of 912 kilometers.

The particulars are as follows: total length of three-coach train, 72,200 mm; pivot distance, 18,000 mm; bogie wheel base, 2,800 mm; wheel diameter, 900 mm; mechanical part weight, 110 tons; tare weight, 136 tons; weight fully laden, 154 tons; maximum axle load, 13.5 tons; manufacturers, ASJ, Kockums, and ASEA. In addition to these vehicles, four-coach units also were ordered, series Xoa8, which originally were supplied to private railway lines but later taken over by the state.

Series Xoa5 contains many interesting design details. Because the trains work in the long and severe Swedish winter, the vehicles have thermal insulation, double-glazing, and air-conditioning. The walls are wood-veneered. Full restaurant and buffet service is provided, with meals served aircraft-fashion at the seats. The four-coach train Xoa8 has a separate restaurant and buffet car.

There is no actual driver's cab, the operator sitting at a kind of console table with instruments and handles placed in a very convenient manner. All doors are opened and closed automatically by the driver. The electrical installation consists, as said before, of four motors. In addition, there is the main, 20-step transformer. Control is by cam-operated gear. Heating is carried out with 40 kw 1,000-v units. The train can be run with multiple-unit control.

In view of the low permitted axle-load, special attention was paid to weight reduction. For example, motor housings are made from an aluminum alloy, silumin, and the motor weighs only 1,350 kg or 4 kg/hp; on maximum output of 2,340 hp, this figure goes down to 2.3 kg/hp. Special filters are provided to protect against snow and dampness. Because of the aluminum housings, nose suspension was substituted by a kind of universal rubber coupling or "quill" drive for power transmission. Roller and silent bloc bearings are used wherever possible. One of the most difficult tasks was the mounting of the main transformer under the coachbody, since the space allowed was only 240 mm above railhead.

Additional Lightweight Trains in Sweden

To compete with ever-increasing air services, a number of three- and four-coach trains were ordered in 1959, series Yoa2, which had the following main dimensions: speed, 105 km/h; wheel diameters, 676

Lightweight motorcoach train, series Yoa2, for Sweden.

mm; distance of bogie centers, 11,900/11,400 mm; and total length of the four-coach train, 69,800 mm. There are two motors (2 x 230 hp = 460 hp) with a transmission ratio of 47:14 or 46:15.

The four-coach train weighs only 79 tons, wherein the outer motor coaches weigh 26 and 21 tons and the trailers, 16 tons. There is a single pantograph, with fuse-protection. The main transformer is housed in one of the end vehicles; all contactor and switch gear is attached to the 10-step transformer. The welded body is itself welded to the underframe, and the steel cover is welded onto the body structure. The trains are attractively painted in red with ornamental lines. Great attention was paid to the bogie design. The motor coaches have both inner axles driven.

Japanese Motor Coaches and Trains

The small Japanese railway companies started to electrify their lines for economic and technical reasons between 1923 and 1930. English Electric and its Japanese associate, Toyo Denki, carried out this work, supplying no less than 520 motor coaches in these years to the lines listed in Table 12.

In general, these vehicles had two motors for the 600-v lines and four for the 1,500-v lines. In addition, locomotives also were supplied. The Japanese State Railway had its first electric line between Ochanomizu and Nakano, 12.5-km-long, which it purchased in 1906 from the Kobu Railway Company. It later formed part of the Shuo line near Tokyo Central Station.

In 1912 came the electrification of the Usui–Pass line. In the years between the two world wars, 126.2 kilometers of the Tokaido line were electrified between Tokyo and Nomazu, as well as two lines of 123.8 and 41.5 kilometers. After World War II, it was first the old Tokaido line that was electrified (366 kilometers between Tokyo and Nagoya).

Current used in 1955 was still D.C. with a wide variety: 600-v (21 kilometers), 750-v (47 kilometers), and 1,200-v (80 kilometers), but mainly 1,500-v (1,727 kilometers). In this year, Japan still only had about 2,000 kilometers of electrified lines. From 1960 onwards, intensive studies were made, and as a result it was decided to electrify until 1975 about 5,500 kilometers, all with 20,000-v and single-phase A.C. of 50 cycles.

Locomotives were to be used mainly for freight traffic, while passenger services were to employ motor coaches and motorcoach trains both for

Dutch motorcoach train set.

Rack locomotive for Ritten Railway for rack section.

Original (1909) motor coach of the Trient–Malé (Malles) Railway, Italy.

Freight motorcoach train for Trient–Malé Railway.

New motorcoach train for Trient–Malé Railway.

Jungfrau Railway: 1955 motorcoach train.

Rack motor coach for the Zugspitz Railway of Bavaria.

Jungfrau Railway: 1912
rack locomotive and
train.

Table 12
JAPANESE MOTOR COACHES

Line	Tension (all D.C.)	H.P.	Number of Vehicles	Line	Tension (all D.C.)	H.P.	Number of Vehicles
Amemiya	600	280	6	Nagoya	600	360	53
Chikuma	1,500	336	6	Nara	1,500	400	27
Hamshin	1,500	400	15	Ome	1,200	240	11
Hanwa	1,500	800	29	Saito Koshi	600	280	4
Hiroshima	1,500	320	5	Shin Keihan	600	130	70
Ikegami	1,500	240	8	Shonan	1,500	320	28
Ise	1,500	400	13	Shizuoka	1,500	320	2
Kagamikahara	600	240	8	Sobu	1,500	380	8
Keihan	600	200	73	Taguchi	1,500	320	3
Keisei	600	288	41	Tanigumi	600	200	6
Kongozan	1,500	240	11	Tobu	1,500	480	75
Mino	600	200	10	Tojokawa	1,500	320	14

1,500-v D.C. motorcoach set for the Ome Tetsudo R.R., Japan, 1928.

Shonan-type motorcoach train, consisting of 10+5 vehicles; four motor coaches and two driving trailers. Built since 1951, Japanese State Railways.

express and suburban work. This plan meant that by 1975 about a third of the Japanese National Railways network would be electrified and this third would carry 75 percent of all traffic.

In the meantime, suitable vehicles were to be developed to run both under D.C. and A.C. systems. There are 50- and 60-cycle systems in different parts of Japan. In 1957, experimental trains were built consisting of a motor coach and trailer in which mercury-arc as well as silicone rectifiers were to be used. Furthermore, a three-coach train consisting of a motor coach and two trailers was built to explore the possibility of using commutator motors. This vehicle had four 8-pole motors with an output of 600 kw; a speed of 110 km/h was reached. Another type, series Kumoya 791-1, built by Kamasaki, was to be used for A.C. traction and was similar to the new Tokaido line.

Because the Japanese had no experience at all with 60-cycle commutator motors, six different types were ordered from six different makers. All motors have an output of 110–150 kw; four motors per train were used and either one or two trailers were to be hauled. The motor coaches are 20,000 mm long, have 108 seats, and weigh 45.2 tons. Maximum speed is 92 km/h. The motor coaches were equipped with repulsion-induction motors for 50-cycle traction. These vehicles, Kumoya 790-1, are 17,000 mm long, have hydraulic power-transmission, and were supplied by Hitachi and Shinko. They proved to be simple and robust vehicles. The motor has an output of 130 kw. A second vehicle, 790-11, has a 134-kw repulsion-induction motor by Mitsubishi and is designed for 100 km/h maximum speed against 70 km/h for type 790-1.

A characteristic example of postwar D.C. work is the Shonan type for 110 km/h. These trains were destined for Tokyo–Hamamatsu line, and they have 15 to 16 trailers, including a mail coach. The vehicles form basic five- and ten-unit trains, the five-unit train having two motors and two driving trailers and the ten-coach train having four motor cars and two driving trailers. The mail and luggage motor van is added at one end. Particulars are listed in Table 13.

Table 13
TOKYO–HAMAMATSU LINE

	Motor Coach	Driving Trailer
Capacity in seats	92	79
Capacity in standees	34	26
Tare weight (tons)	47	31
Total length (mm)	20,000	20,000
1-hour output (kw) at	500	—
km/h	63	—
Gear Ratio	1:2.56	

The "New Tokaido" Line and its Vehicles, Japan

In 1964, the so-called New Tokaido line of the Japanese State Railways was opened. The line connects Japan's two most important cities, Tokyo and

Express train for the "New Tokaido" line, 200 km/h, Japan.

Osaka, 515 kilometers apart. It is the first Japanese standard-gauge line, and uses 25,000-v single-phase A.C. of 60 cycles with a traveling speed of 200 km/h, bringing the results of the above-mentioned experiments to fruition.

The line was badly needed, as the old Tokaido line with 122 passenger and 78 freight trains per day had reached its limit of capacity. On the new line, motorcoach trains travel at half-hour intervals. The trains have twelve coaches, all axles being motorized and the motors having an output of 185 kw/1-hour. Every two vehicles form a close-coupled unit. Thirty trains were ordered, with a seating capacity of 987. The two-coach unit thus has eight axles and eight motors of 1,480-kw output.

Motors are arranged in a series of four and each group of four is in parallel. The main transformer has an output of 1,650 KVA; the current then goes to silicone rectifiers that supply pulsating alternating current. Main technical details are as follows: gear ratio, 1:2.17; pivot distance, 17,500 mm; bogie wheel base, 2,500 mm; wheel diameter, 910 mm; total length, 25,000 mm. The whole electrical installation is positioned under the floor, and the vehicles are designed as a welded self-supporting tube, using lightweight materials.

There are super-express trains (Hikari) and express trains (Kodama). The 515-km-long line is traversed in three and four hours, with two intermediate stops. Freight trains travel at night. The old Tokaido line is being used for local traffic and slow freight trains. The new Tokaido line is such a success that a third one is being built, although there is strong environmental opposition, because the trains are very noisy and disturb the foundations of neighboring buildings.

The Lightweight Motor Coaches of the Pennsylvania Railroad, Type "Pioneer III," U.S.A.

In 1957, the Pennsylvania Railroad ordered several vehicles from the Budd firm in a determined attempt to create a truly modern lightweight vehicle. This vehicle was sought as an answer to ever-increasing air and auto competition, which especially in the United States has reduced passenger traffic on the rails substantially. The vehicles were termed Pioneer III, and were to weigh only about 24 tons, or 27.5 kg per passenger. Budd, which specialized in building lightweight vehicles for the aircraft and railway industries, applied these experiences and technologies in Pioneer III. The vehicle had four axles and carried 88 passengers. It had the following main dimensions: total length, 25,970 mm; distance of bogie centers, 18,065 mm; bogie wheel base, 1,990 mm; total weight, 23.8 tons; wheel diameter, 760 mm. Pioneer III proved to be a failure.

"Pioneer III" suburban train set of the Pennsylvania Railroad (built by Budd).

"TEE" five-coach train set, series RAe II of the SBB; wheel arrangement 2'2'+(A1A)(A1A)+2'2'+2'2'+2'2'.

The Electric Trans-European Express Trains of the SBB (TEE Train)

Since 1957, the leading western and central European railways have introduced a new international transport system (SNCF, SNCB, DB, SBB, NS, FS, and OeBB). Novel, modern, and fast express train links with great comfort were developed to connect the main cities of Europe and stop the growing competition of road and air by beating both in speed, safety, and comfort. The first trains were diesel-driven, and, since 1961, electric units have been supplied under the leadership of the SBB that can run under the following four current systems:

1. 15,000-v, 16⅔ cycles, single-phase A.C.: DB, OeBB, SBB

2. 25,000-v, 50 cycles, single-phase A.C.: SNCF
3. 1,500-v D.C.: SNCF, NS
4. 3,000-v, D.C.: FS, SNCB

The trains, called TEE (Trans-European Expresses) have five to six coaches and are mostly run as twin units with 10 to 12 vehicles. In the beginning, the Basel–Zurich–Milan–Paris run was made; TEE was later extended to all leading European centers and can run under all European electric lines.

The vehicles for the trains were supplied by SIG-Neuhausen, the electrical part by MFO, and the air-conditioning by BBC. The coaches of a five- to six-unit train consist of the following: at each train end is a driving trailer, one to two inner trailers, a dining car, and an engine car. The middle coaches

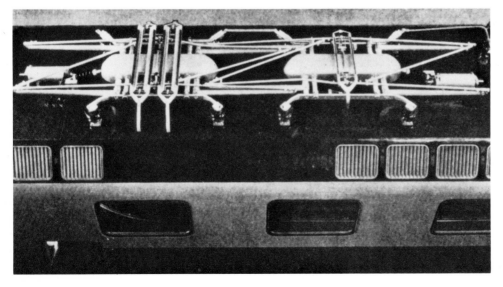

"TEE" five-coach train set; pantograph layout for all four main European current systems.

each contain a large compartment with 42 seats. Vehicles are built as modern self-supporting tubular structures and are connected by concertina links. The coaches are acoustically and thermally well insulated. All components were carefully investigated, tested, and built.

The engine car contains the equipment necessary for running under four different current systems, as well as kitchen and service quarters. The transformer, the heaviest part, is positioned in the center of the vehicle, which is 24,200 mm long. The body rests on two to three axle bogies, the outer axles being motorized. Power-transmission is carried out by BBC spring drive. The center axle is a running axle.

All wheels are of the monobloc type and have a 1,100-mm diameter. To reduce wear, an automatic, electropneumatic, tire-grease device is used. The frame is an all-welded hollow-bar construction that contains all cables and ventilating equipment. The body has torsion-bar suspension; it rests on four points on V-shaped silent blocs on a pendulum cradle. The latter rests with spherical bearings on the end of the torsion bars; each axle box has two pendulum roller bearings.

The electrical installation had to be designed to satisfy the requirements of all four current systems and to enable the train to cover the steepest ascents of the Gotthard and Simplon lines (26‰) and Arlberg (33‰). Four motors were selected that are

Main circuit diagram for "TEE" train set.

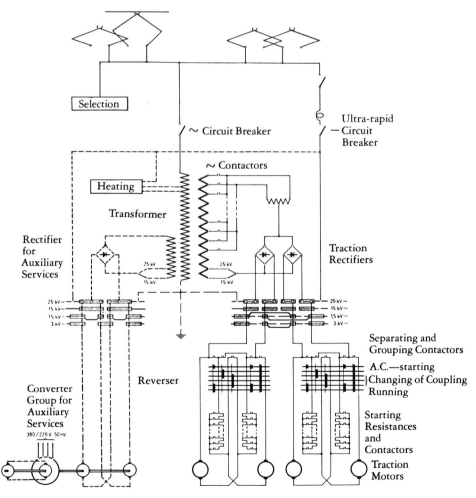

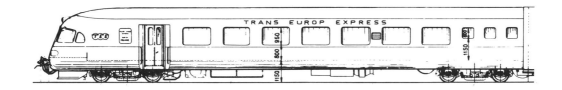

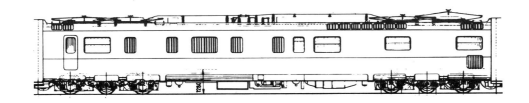

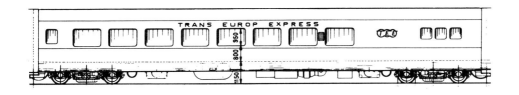

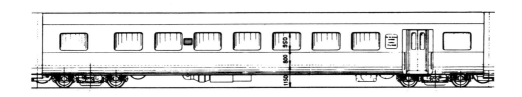

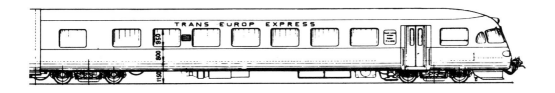

ELECTRIC "TEE" TRAIN
SERIES RAe 1051–1054 (FIVE UNITS), SBB

DRIVING WHEEL DIAMETER: 1110 MM
RUNNING WHEEL DIAMETER: 940 MM
GEAR RATIO: 1:2.34
NO. OF MOTORS: 4
TOTAL TRAIN WEIGHT: 259 T
ADHESIVE WEIGHT OF MOTOR COACH: 68 T

SEATS: 126
SEATS IN DINER & BAR: 48 + 6 = 54
MAX. TRACTIVE EFFORT: 16,000 KG
MAX SPEED: 160 KM/H
BUILDING YEAR: 1961

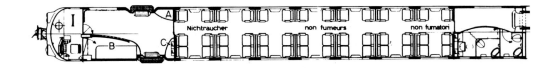

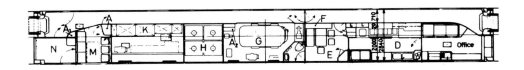

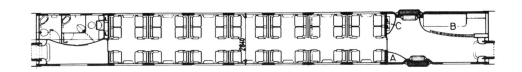

A: MACHINERY COMPARTMENT
B: LUGGAGE & CLOAK ROOM
C: AIR CONDITIONING
D: KITCHEN
E: PERSONNEL ROOM
F: PNEUMATIC EQUIPMENT
G: TRANSFORMER

H: RESISTANCES
K: RECTIFIER
L: AIR CHANNELS
M: CUSTOMERS & TRAIN PERSONNEL
N: LUGGAGE ROOM: 2.5 M²/T
P: GUARD

used in A.C. traction with main transformers and silicone rectifiers; in D.C. traction, they are used directly from the catenary over resistances.

The pantographs had to be very carefully laid out, since the pressure and currents vary for A.C. and D.C. traction; there are also differences in standard heights to overcome. Four pantographs were installed after tests at BBC; they are arranged in pairs and their specifications are in Table 14.

Motors, auxiliaries, and control systems are switched according to the type of current being used. For this purpose, an electropneumatic rotary contactor with four positions was developed, carefully protected by fail-safe devices. As mentioned, the

Table 14
SPECIFICATIONS OF TEE TRAINS

Pantograph	Number of Contacts	Contact Width (mm)	System	Pressure (kg) at km/h V=0	V=160
1	2	1,950	SNCF	9	16
2	1	1,450	SNCF, FS	8	12
3	1	1,320	SBB	7	9
4	2	1,950	SNCB, NS, OeBB	9	16

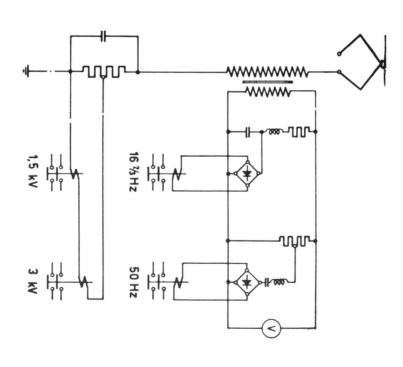

Traction system selector and current diagram for "TEE" train set.

motors can be supplied with current in two different ways.

In D.C. traction, the current is supplied to a D.C. ultra-rapid circuit breaker, then to a traction-system commutator, and from there to the starting resistances and motors. The motors work in two groups; these are first connected in series and then in parallel. The starting resistances are bridged over, and then there are four field-reduction steps, where the movements are carried out in bridge connection. At 1,500-v tension, the two motor groups are permanently connected in parallel, and, at 3,000-v, permanently in series. The changeover is carried out by the traction-system contactor.

In A.C. traction, the motors of each group are permanently coupled in parallel, and the traction-system contactor connects each group to a silicone rectifier. These are in their A.C. side connected in parallel with the secondary regulator winding of the transformers. The primary is connected in the usual manner by the circuit breaker to the pantographs. For rectification of the 1-phase current, silicone rectifiers supplied by SSW are used. Per branch of Graetz connection, seven diodes are in series and four are connected in parallel. The transformer has a constant output of 2,592 KVA of $16\frac{2}{3}$ cycles, or 3,375 KVA at 50 cycles.

The trains are braked electrically to allow them to run downhill on any existing gradient at constant speed. The motors are then used as D.C. generators. Other main dimensions are as follows:

Total length of five-coach train: 125,300 mm
Total length of motor coach: 24,200 mm
Seating arrangements: 126 + 48 (dining car) + 6 (bar)
Wheel diameters—driving wheels: 1,100 mm
　　　　　　　　—running wheels: 940 mm
Total weight: 259 tons
Maximum speed: 160 km/h
Maximum output: 2,376 kw/h
Maximum tractive effort: 16,000 kg
Type of service (voltage): $16\frac{2}{3}$ cycles A.C., 50 cycles A.C., 1,500 D.C., 3,000 D.C.
Output (kw/1-hour): 2,376, 2,376, 2,272, 2,272
Tractive effort (kg): 9,700　　　9,500
(at kw/h):　　　　87.5　　　85

The "Blue Trains" of Glasgow, Scotland

With about one million inhabitants, Glasgow is the most important city in Scotland. The early railway history in and around the city was filled with the bitter struggles of the early railway companies until the 1923 Amalgamation Act allocated the districts south of the Clyde to the LMS Railway and the ones north of the Clyde to the LNER. This led to considerable improvements, but even so it was a difficult and awkward system until the railways were fully united under British Railways.

The B.R. developed a completely new railway system in which electrification of the suburban lines

"Blue Trains" for suburban sections, Glasgow, B.R.

played a decisive part. Airdrie–Glasgow–Helensburgh via Singer and Yoker were electrified, as were the Cathcart, Kirkhill, and Neilston lines. The whole district is densely populated and industrialized, but it also has a substantial tourist traffic because the lines reach into the Scottish lake district.

Electrification work started in 1957 and took four years. The technical problems to be solved were very substantial, since many of the lines literally had to be rebuilt. The rails in most tunnels had to be laid at lower levels to allow for electrification. Most stations needed rebuilding. In addition, a modern color-light signaling system was introduced.

The new vehicles, painted a strong blue, are arranged as three-coach trains and can be run in multiple units as six- and nine-coach trains. The outer vehicles have drivers' cabs and the center vehicle is motorized. The electrification encompassed 83 kilometers north and 29 kilometers south of the Clyde. Originally 25,000-v single-phase A.C. was used, to be reduced on town sections to 6,500-v, but the changeover led to great difficulties and the idea was abandoned.

Electric Motor Coaches in South Africa

The first important line in South Africa to be electrified was the main line connecting the Transvaal with Durban—the link between Glencoe and Pieter-

maritzburg. This took place in 1935 and used 3,000-v D.C. The electrification used mainly locomotives, but essential suburban services near Johannesburg, the "Reef" lines, also were electrified. After early locomotive traction, the 1935 electrification also comprised 72 four-motor 1,500/3,000-v motor coaches with only one driver's cab. In addition, 32 driving trailers and 128 trailers were ordered; the contracts were subsequently increased to 119, 80, and 235 units respectively. The electrical installations were purchased in England and put into locally built vehicles in South Africa.

In 1948, another 54 train sets were ordered for the Reef lines. The 4-axle vehicles (all using 1,067 mm gauge) were fully motorized and had four 310-hp nose-suspended motors working with 1,500-v D.C., two of each motor being permanently coupled in series. The motors can be operated in series, series-parallel, and parallel connection with field-weakening position. All high-tension equipment is contained in a separate chamber; the resistances are under the coach floor. Each motorcoach train consists of two motor coaches and six trailers, or three motor coaches and eight trailers. Each motor coach has two pantographs and electropneumatic contactor gear.

In 1952, the Cape lines were electrified with 3,000-v D.C., and subsequently all 1,500-v lines were converted to 3,000-v D.C. Between 1952 and 1958, 78 motor coaches were ordered, and in 1955 an additional 105 motor coaches and 244 trailers for the

Motor coach for the "Reef" electrification in the Transvaal, South African State Railways.

Two-story motor coach for New South Wales Railways.

Reef (Johannesburg) sections were requested. In 1960, another substantial order followed when the AEI firm supplied 113 four-coach train sets that were to be used both for the Capetown (Cape) and Johannesburg (Reef) sections. The 78 units previously mentioned had all-steel bodies, forming a tubular unit with the underframe. Motors had a 1-hour output of 315 hp and transmitted power with a gear ratio of 17:65. The motors again were coupled in pairs in series and controlled by an electropneumatic contactor gear. Seating capacity was 96.

Two-story Motor Coaches for the New South Wales Government Railways of Australia

This railway ordered four different two-story motor coaches with one two-floor trailer each. The vehicles have a single pantograph at one end, while the other end contains the driver's cab and a crew room. The high-tension installations such as resistances and main switch are fixed on the roof. Other electrical installations are housed in a separate chamber at the coach end.

The driver's cab is carefully laid out and experimental types were developed for standing or sitting drivers. Three of the vehicles have air-springing, and, in the fourth, the U.S. Pioneer III system was used. (See previous section.) In addition, various types of nose-suspended motors were tested. The contactor-gear is electropneumatic. The vehicles are 20,317 mm long, and pivot distance is 13,945 mm. The vehicles were built in Australia, and the electrical installations were bought from Mitsubishi, Toshiba, Hitachi, and English Electric.

The Electrification of the Brazilian Central Railways

This railway is state-owned and runs from Rio de Janeiro to São Paulo, a distance of about 600 kilometers, forming the main line of the country. Because of very substantial commuter traffic, plans existed for many years to improve services and electrify the line. This was realized in 1937 when a group of British companies supplied the entire installation.

The line has 5-foot, 3-inch gauge (1,676 mm) and uses 3,000-v D.C. Initially, about 180 kilometers of rail length were converted. Sixty three-coach trains were ordered, consisting of a central motor coach and two driving trailers. In multiple-unit control, one, two, and three such trains can be run together.

Vehicles were of all-steel construction, and were well designed and insulated against the hot climate. Each motor coach with driver's cab had two fully motorized 2-axle bogies. The four 4-pole motors of 175-hp output were the nose-suspended type; they were coupled in pairs in series and used 1,500-v D.C.

7,000-v D.C. 800-hp motor coach for Rio-São Paulo, Brazil.

Bogie for Brazilian motor coach.

Wheel diameter is 970 mm and gear ratio, 18:71. Other main dimensions are: length, 19,980 mm; pivot distance, 14,335 mm; and bogie wheel base, 2,590/2,000 mm. The vehicles can accommodate 200 to 220 passengers, 68 to 72 of them sitting. Weight in working order is 56/34 tons.

The electrification was such a great success that it was decided to extend the electric system. In 1948, 30 more trains were ordered, identical to the original 60, and in 1949 another 20 were ordered. After careful investigations, an additional 50 three-coach trains and also 50 motor coaches were ordered from Metro-Vickers, which furnished the electrical installations, and local firms, which provided the bodywork.

These trains, supplied during 1956/57, can be combined with the earlier ones in multiple-unit service. The new vehicles follow the latest ideas in railway vehicle construction and are built in self-supporting steel construction. They have four motors of 318 hp/1-hour output; control is by electro-pneumatic contactor gear, whereby all electrical installations are placed under the coach floor.

The Electrification of the Suburban Lines of Buenos Aires

Buenos Aires is not only the largest city in the Southern Hemisphere but, with its 5.5 million inhabitants, one of the largest in the world. Originally, the transport system was partly in the possession of city authorities and partly owned by a British-Argentinian group of companies that ran the underground railway and the central Argentinian railway, which connects the town center with some larger settlements, such as Tigre. Another line, which served the western suburbs, was the Buenos Aires Western Railway. Both lines have broad gauge (1,676 mm).

The BAW Railway, opened in 1857, is the oldest Argentinian railway; it was taken over by the English group in 1890. To improve suburban traffic, it was decided in 1913 to electrify these sections. World War I severely delayed progress, and only in 1923 was Tigre reached, comprising 37 kilometers and a connecting line to the port.

Service began with 46 motor coaches, 45 driving trailers, and one other vehicle. Metropolitan-Vickers

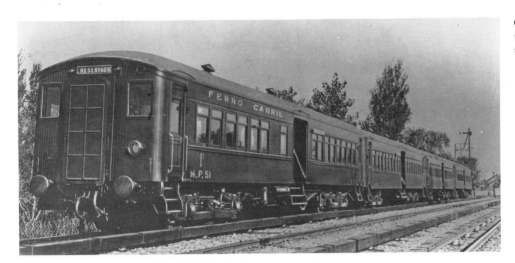

Original design of motorcoach trains for the Buenos Aires suburban lines, Argentina.

carried out the work and later received additional contracts for 76 motor coaches and 97 driving trailers. All lines were electrified with 800-v D.C. and third rail. Each motor coach has two drivers' cabs, and all four axles are motorized with 4 x 200-hp motors. The driving trailers have only one cab. All sliding contacts are connected and form a power line. The vehicles use electromagnetic contactor gear and multiple-unit control. All electrical installations are contained in dust-proof cases under the floor.

Another line that electrified its suburban services was the Central Argentine Railway. Originally, 70 route and 147 rail kilometers were converted. Electric services started in 1916 and two more lines were converted in 1929, the system being the same as before—800-v D.C. and third rail.

In the beginning, 55 motor coaches were ordered, all fully motorized with 2 x 250-hp nose-suspended motors; in addition, 50 driving trailers were ordered, later followed by 111 motor coaches, 75 driving trailers, and 95 trailers. The original vehicles were 19,825 mm long and had wooden bodies; the later ones had steel bodies and were 21,350 mm long. The newer vehicles have two 310-hp motors with electromagnetic control gear, with electrical installations again fixed under the car floor. All installations were supplied by British firms.

Part 2

History of the Electric Industrial Locomotive

Electric industrial locomotives are used in certain major fields of activity, as, for example, in (1) underground mines, where narrow space determines the design and size of the locomotive, but where essential features are fire safety and reliability, (2) in steel and metal works where large quantities of raw materials have to be moved over short distances quickly and frequently, and (3) in modern industrial organizations. The most important use for electric industrial locomotives has been in open-cast mining, such as the gigantic lignite mines in Eastern Germany, and also in many mining organizations around the world, such as in Australia and the Congo (Zaire).

The Electric Underground Mining Locomotive

In underground mining, the electric locomotive, using mainly overhead catenary systems, has reached a leading position for the past 40 years. Originally, the gauges used varied between 450 mm and 700 mm, with outputs of 30–50 kw and weights of 5–7 tons. As mining railways lengthened, larger freight vehicles were introduced that needed much more powerful locomotives, up to 200 kw. The locomotives are almost always 2-axled with two motors. Where their effort was insufficient, twin units were introduced that could be controlled from one driver's cab. Efficient forced-air ventilating systems contributed to improved outputs.

For areas that are in danger of spontaneous combustion, battery locomotives (with 150-v battery tension) were introduced. In addition, dual types exist where the locomotive works off the catenary in safe areas and off the battery in danger zones. A typical vehicle of this type has an output of 40 kw/1-hour at 150-v battery tension and 60 kw/1-hour at 220-v catenary voltage.

The size and weight of the engine depends very much on the size and capacity of the lifting devices, since these have to take the locomotive underground to its place of work. In addition, the size of the mine workings has to be considered. In the case of newly developed mines, the task, of course, is much easier than in already-existing mines; modern practice also has followed much stricter rules for safety and servicing, since the height of the wires is rarely more than 1,600–1,800 mm above rail and there remains, after deducting the necessary space for the pantograph, little more than a 1,000–1,200 mm height for the locomotive. Current used is normally supplied in the form of two T-irons fixed to the roof and on which glides a contact shoe.

The First Electric Mining Locomotives

Three years after Werner von Siemens showed in an 1879 exhibition in Berlin the first practical electric locomotive, a coal mine in Saxony, the Zauckerode mine, purchased an electric mining locomotive. This

First electric mining locomotive, Zaukerode Mine, 1889.

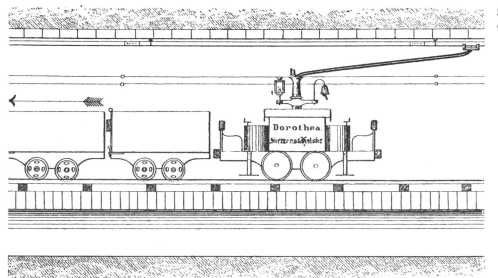

Schematic layout for first electric mining locomotive.

locomotive worked without interruption for 45 years, was withdrawn in 1927, and is displayed in the Siemens Works Museum in Berlin.

Other mining works followed, such as the Hohenzollern mine in Silesia and the saltworks in New Stassfurt. In America, the first electric mining locomotive was supplied for the Lykens Valley mine in Pennsylvania. This locomotive weighed about 6 tons and could haul about a 100-ton load; speed was 10 km/h. The distance to overcome was 5 kilometers and the maximum gradient was 15‰. Voltage was 400-v. Power-transmission was by chain drive and wheel diameter was 760 mm. A similar locomotive

for the Erie mine in Pennsylvania was built in 1889; it had a 40-hp motor, also for 400-v; its weight was 5 tons.

The construction of mining locomotives naturally followed not only the legal and commercial requirements but also the general technical developments of locomotive design. The locomotive body was first made from cast iron and later cast steel; next came riveted and finally welded frames. Development of electric motors and control installations occurred in much the same way in most industrialized countries. A typical example of the period from the late 1800s to 1910 is the 1889 locomotive

Original and rebuilt motor coach of the
Bernina Railway, now also used on
Chur–Arosa line.

Motor coach of D.R., series ET91,
with glass roof for tourist services.

Motorcoach train Z.5100/ZS.15100 for suburban
services of Paris (Melun and Chartres) made from
stainless steel and built in 1954.

Rack-and-adhesion motor coach ABe 4/4 for Rhaetian Railway.

Motor coach for RABDe
12/12 of the SBB.

Motor coach of the Vitznau–
Rigi Railway of 1950–56.

Motorcoach train for the Centovalli Railway, 1959.

Motor coach of 1907 of the Valle Maggia Railway.

Motorcoach train of the Ritten
(Renon) Railway, near Bozen
(Bolzano), Italy.

Mining locomotive of 1889, 40 hp 220-v, for Erie Mine, Pennsylvania.

Standard American mining locomotive of 1895, built by General Electric Co., showing progress made in about 20 years.

illustrated. This 4-ton locomotive, built by General Electric Company, had a cable-drum to carry an extra 100–150-m double-trailing cable to haul wagons in nonelectrified mining areas. Other main dimensions are shown in the illustration.

In a review published in 1957, the BBC-Mannheim firm showed typical examples of mining locomotives for the period 1930–60. Their five illustrations clearly demonstrate the design trends and the difficulty in designing locomotives for the widely varying profiles of mines. One of the locomotives had an unusual drive; it used a 1-phase A.C. 50 Hz motor of 250-v and had a Deri-motor, fixed rigidly in the frame, which transmitted momentum by a gear train/cardan shaft and conical gears to one axle, while the other axle was driven directly by a chain drive.

To appreciate the developments of the last 10–15 years, consider a modern mining locomotive built by AEG. According to the requirements of the

Bo' 220-v D.C. mining locomotive of 1939, BBC-Mannheim, 550-mm gauge, 8 tons, 2 x 18 kw/1-hour.

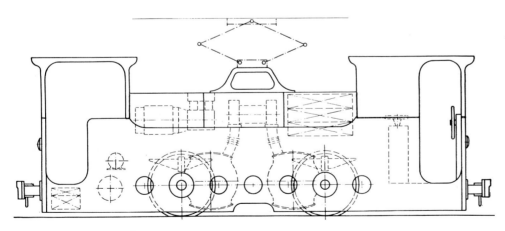

Mining locomotive for German coal mine; built as a single unit with force-ventilated motors, air compressor, and light generator.

Driving control: Monopolar
Hourly performance: 2 × 45 kw by 600 v
Weight: 15 tons
Track Breadth: 600 mm
Locomotive width: 1400 mm
Height of driver's cab: 1970 mm
Lowest position of overhead electrical system: 2400 mm

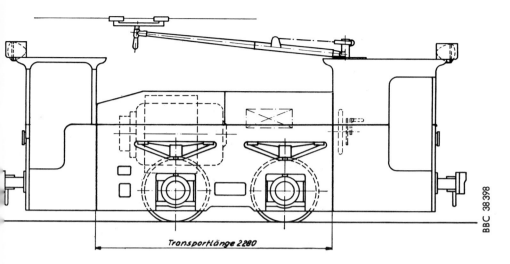

Mining locomotive for iron ore mine in West Germany. Driver's cab and worker's room can be separated for transport purposes down the mineshaft.

Transportlange = Carriage length

Driving Control: Bipolar
Hourly Performance: 1 × 40 kw with single phase sinusoidal alternating current (250v, 50Hz)
Weight: 7.5 tons
Track Breadth: 680 mm
Locomotive Width: 960 mm
Height of Driver's Cab: 1600 mm
Lowest position of overhead electrical system: 2000 mm
Carriage dimensions of the largest portion: length × width × height = 2,280 × 960 × 840 mm

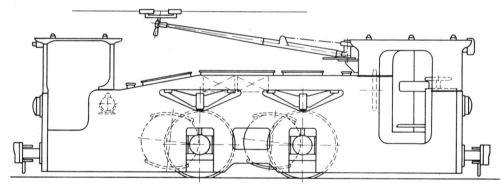

Mining locomotive for German iron ore mine, built as a single unit. The body can be used for two different locomotive types: 70/80 kw or 40 kw.

Driving Control: Bipolar
Hourly Performance: 2 × 18 kw with 220 v
Weight: 12 tons
Track Breadth: 600 mm
Locomotive Width: 1000 mm
Height of Driver's Cab: 1500 mm
Lowest position of overhead electrical system: 1800 mm

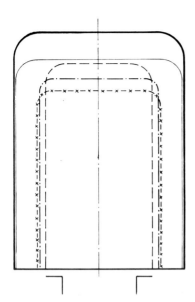

A cross-section comparison of different mine locomotives.

_ _ _ _ = the Ewald-König Ludwig local of the Bergbau association

•_•_•_•_ = the Phannenberger local of the Erzbergbau association

–x–x–x–x– = the Nammen mine of the Barbara Erzbergbau association

_____ = the Friedrichshall works of the Kali-Chemie association

_____ = the Herfa-Neurode works of the Wintershall association

Comparative line profiles for different mining locomotives.

Industrial locomotive with Deri motor and drive.

user, these are locomotives for catenary work without explosion protection; compound locomotives for work in safe or (with battery drive) unsafe conditions; and, also as battery locomotives, for work only in dangerous areas.

According to modern practice and mining regulations, overhead wires may be used only where there are fully ventilated mines; under no circumstances may they be used in the actual coal-cutting area. The overhead-line locomotives are obviously more desirable, since they can travel greater distances than battery locomotives, which are severely limited in their area of operation. In addition, they are immediately ready for use and can be substantially overloaded.

Gauge today is mostly between 500–700 mm. The 1-hour output is 50–120 kw, and weights can vary between 8 and 22 tons. The danger of accidentally touching the catenary is reduced by a 2-pole installation or a single-pole one covered with timber protection. The current collectors are usually gliding shoes.

Open-cast mining locomotive for the Victoria State Electricity Commission, Victoria, Australia, 1957.

Open-cast Mining Locomotives: Developments between 1900 and 1950

One of the most important uses of industrial electric locomotives is in the field of open-cast mining, especially of brown coal (lignite) mining in East Germany and Poland. These enormous mines, of mountain-like size, were only modestly exploited by 1900. Demand was limited to the amounts of coal that could be hauled, and the length and depth of the haul were very modest. But with ever-increasing demands, it was necessary to extend the mining areas into greater depths and increased output. In 1930, consumption of brown coal was four times that of 1900; by 1943 it was sixfold.

The means of transport were mostly 900-mm gauge railways, rarely the more expensive standard gauge. Current used was 600-v D.C., and the tractive effort rarely exceeded 10 tons. From about 1930 onwards, a new era of development followed: D.C. of 1,200- to 1,500-v was used, locomotives weighed up to 75 tons, and motors had outputs up to 2,000 hp. Standard gauge was used and the tractive effort increased to about 20 tons.

From 1950 onwards, a third period of development began to take place. Now locomotives were required to satisfy very high standards of design and output. Remote control with removal of the overburden by mechanical means was developed. Working depths reached up to 250 m, and train weights of up to 2,000 tons had to be moved.

These demands brought about the appearance of powerful and unusual types of locomotives. These newly designed locomotives weigh up to 150 tons and have 2,000 hp output. They have to work on rails that are rarely well and carefully laid down and have to overcome gradients of up to 35‰. A further problem was created by the ever-increasing efficiency of the excavating machinery. In 1900, these were about 500 m³/hr and 50 years later reached no less than 7,000 m³/hr.

Between 1900 and 1930, locomotives were mostly 4-axled, with 2 bogies, and weighed 40–60 tons, with an axle load of about 15 tons. Output per motor axle was about 200 hp, while voltage rose from 500- to 1,200-v D.C. The locomotives were of simple and robust design. First there was a riveted steel frame, and later heavy plate frames. The typical form had a central driver's cab, lowered between the bogies to go through the opening space of the excavating machine.

A 4-axle Bo-Bo locomotive built by SSW in 1912 is a typical example. It weighed 46 tons, had 900-mm gauge, and an output of 88 kw per axle. Nose-suspended motors were used, and control was by slip-ring controller.

When output rose to 1,500 m³/h, far more powerful locomotives were needed. A 4-axled locomotive, built by SSW and Henschel in 1930, weighing about 75 tons and having 900-mm gauge, almost became a standard design. It had an output of 4 x 185 kw/h and 1,200-v D.C. current.

Four-axled 46-ton mining locomotive, Bo'-Bo' 900-mm gauge, 400 kw, 600-v.

Four-axled mining locomotive, 1,435-mm gauge, weighing 100 tons, and having 1,500 kw, 1,200-v.

Newly developed mining installations began to use standard gauge with permitted axle loads up to 25 tons. They weighed about 100 tons, had the wheel arrangement Bo'-Bo', and had an output of 4 x 350 kw at 1,500-v D.C.

However, output increased further, and, before World War II, Bo'-Bo'-Bo' locomotives were built. This 1938 design had three sections, the end parts connected by triangular couplings with the middle part. They were very successful since they ran safely over badly laid rails and proved very maneuverable in the many and narrow curves.

The 900-mm gauge Bo'-Bo' locomotive weighed, as stated, 75 tons and had four nose-suspended motors of 185 kw/h. With the framewalls and cross-members, the whole body produces a solid, power-transmitting unit. The frame was cranked, and the simple and rugged construction proved very satisfactory under onerous working conditions.

On the fixed approach-lines, the current is collected by two standard pantographs, but for use on temporary lines within the actual mine-workings, four side-collectors are provided. These pantographs are hand-operated by cable by the driver and can be

Bo'-Bo'-Bo' open-cast mining locomotive for the Otto Scharf mine, built in 1938.

locked when not in use. From the pantographs, current goes by a main switch to a step-controller of 18 series and 18 parallel steps. In addition, there are 15 steps for the resistance brake.

A simple axle-load equalizer is built in to improve adhesive weight on badly laid lines. There also is a Leonard switch to allow remote control by the Leonard system. Further particulars were: length, 13,920 mm; bogie center distance, 7,360 mm; bogie wheel base, 2,000 mm; wheel diameter, 950 mm. An example of this type of engine is the open-cast mining locomotive for the Victorian State Electricity Commission.

A typical example of the later Bo'-Bo'Bo' locomotive is the open-cast locomotive for the Otto Scharf mine. The 150-ton locomotive was designed for standard gauge and 1,200-v D.C. catenary voltage. However, the demands for brown coal kept increasing. In Germany alone, 211.5 million tons were produced in 1938, excluding the removal of overburden. The size of the task can be estimated, since the overburden removed was 367 million m³ or 715 million tons.

For this reason, the illustrated 6-axle locomotive was developed for the Otto Scharf mine. Built by SSW and Henschel, it was at that time the biggest open-cast mining locomotive in the world. Temporary rails were simply laid on the ground and moved forward as required. Assuming an excavator output of 2,500 m³/h—with temporary laid rails for a distance of 2–3 kilometers and gradients of 14‰—the load to be hauled was about 1,350 tons, requiring four 150-ton locomotives.

The triangular coupling avoided side movements but permitted vertical adjustments. The frame was riveted to be more elastic, since the frame walls were made of 38-mm-thick plate. Axle load was 25

tons and the six driving motors transmitted their power with a gear ratio of 13:64. The center part carried the driver's cab with two opposing driving positions. The controller was arranged in the center and had two handwheels so that the driver could change places.

The six motors, force-ventilated, were nose-suspended and arranged in three groups of two motors each. The step-controller had eleven series and seven parallel steps, plus field weakening. In addition, there was an electric resistance brake and installations for remote control and slow motion. Other data were: weight of mechanical part, 118 tons, of which ballast was 36 tons; electrical part, 32 tons; driving wheel diameter, 1,050 mm; total wheel base, 13,700 mm; total length, 18,800 mm; 1-hour tractive effort, 22,000 kg at 23.4 km/h; and maximum speed, 60 km/h.

Heavy Rotary Converter and Rectifier Open-cast Mining Locomotives for the Rhenish Brown Coal Industry

Between 1945 and 1950, the BBC, AEG, and SSW firms developed very novel heavy electric locomotives using the single-phase A.C. system for the Rhenish open-cast coal mining industry. On the connecting and shunting lines, the locomotives haul 2,000-ton trains on gradients up to 30‰. Rotary converter locomotives were ordered, as well as rectifier locomotives.

The permanently laid lines are 32 kilometers long and connect the various works and mining areas. Some of the mines reach a depth of 250 m and have inclines of several kilometers long with 30‰

gradients. Because excavators have an output of 100,000 m³ per day, a 240-ton locomotive was required to move these enormous quantities.

Consequently, twin-locomotives with recuperative braking were developed. The trains were remote-controlled from the excavator to avoid spillage or spoil of coal during loading. The design finally chosen had the following main data: total length, 14,500 mm; pivot distance, 6,300 mm; bogie wheel base, 3,200 mm; wheel diameter, 1,120 mm; axle load, 30 tons; and gauge, 1,435 mm.

The rotary converter locomotives have the wheel arrangement Bo'-Bo' and a girder frame that transmits all tractive forces. Only on one front side are there two drivers' cabs, left and right, to allow the driver to change sides. Behind the cabs is the engine room.

Electrical installations include a main transformer for each locomotive. A single-phase motor has characteristics of 1,500 kw–2,000 kw/5 min and cos ϕ = 1, as well as a D.C. converter generator of 1,600 kw output at 760-v. This converter unit receives the catenary voltage of 1-phase A.C. of 6,000-v, 50 Hz on its primary. The current converter is a twin-bearing unit, so that motor and motor generator have a common shaft; they run at 1,500 rpm.

The main rectifier is driven by the synchronous motor; in order to reduce the voltage drop in the catenary to a minimum, the cos ϕ factor is regulated accordingly. Furthermore, the synchronous motor has a 380-v, 3-phase auxiliary winding for the auxiliary services. The four driving motors have an output of 370 kw each, at 760-v, and are arranged in parallel. Additional electrical installations are protection services for the generator. Change of direction is carried by a special contactor. Because there is one contactor for slow motion and remote control, an auxiliary rectifier is used for excitation of the main rectifier.

The twin cabs are so designed that by change of position of the driver, no additional switching operations are required. This procedure is carried out through a set of gear-driven shafts and a control unit on the main (driving) controller. In twin-traction, both vehicles are electrically coupled. In the driving

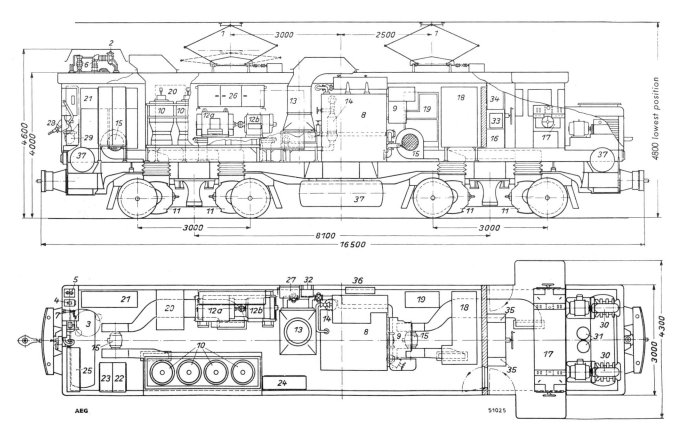

Bo'-Bo' rectifier locomotive, 6,000-v, 50-cycle A.C., built by BBC and Krauss-Maffei.

Outline of Bo'-Bo' rectifier locomotive.

Bo'-Bo' rectifier locomotive with train of self-discharge wagons.

controller, all installations for selection of type of drive, direction, and movement (driving or braking) are combined. In addition, the driving controller contains a selector for the operation of the two main and four auxiliary pantographs, as well as two separate collector regulators for the first (driving) and second (hauled) locomotive. For direction purposes, ultra-short-wave receivers are provided, with an aerial on the cab roof.

To control the train remotely while it is being loaded under the excavator, the driver turns the controller to zero and turns on the slow-motion switch and the rail or excavator switch. The latter provides the short-wave receiver with the correct frequency from the excavator, so that from then on all switching procedures can be controlled from the excavator. Then follows the journey over the weighing machine (all trains have to be weighed). This is done at 0.6 to 0.8 km/h in Leonard drive. The maximum tractive effort is no less than 80,000 kg.

For comparative purposes, rectifier locomotives were ordered in addition to the converter locomotive. The former have a somewhat better degree of efficiency and are, as well, lighter and simpler. It was also hoped that experience would be gained with this type of locomotive in the areas of operation, regenerative braking, grid load, and interference and cooling. The main data of the rectifier locomotives are as follows:

Total length: 16,500 mm
Distance of pivot centers: 8,100 mm

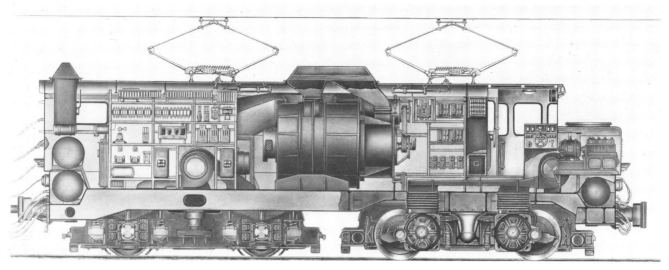

Sectional view of 50-c converter-locomotive for open-cast brown coal mining.

Secondary pantograph for Bo'-Bo' rectifier locomotive.

Wheel diameter: 1,120 mm
Bogie wheel base: 3,100 mm
Axle load: 33 tons
Gauge: 1,435 mm
Weight of mechanical part: 88.5 tons
Weight of electrical part: 43.5 tons
1-hour output of the four motors: 4 x 370 kw
    at 760-v
Gear ratio: 79:14
1-hour tractive effort: 21,600 kg at 24.4 km/h
Maximum starting tractive effort: 43,000 kg
Maximum speed: 70 km/h

Because the trains are to be remotely controlled during loading and stay within a speed range of 0–40 meters per minute, grid-controlled, single-anode rectifiers (excitrons) are used. The motors have series-connection and are suitable for three traction methods: driving, braking, and slow-motion.

Again, two main pantographs are provided in addition to four side-collectors; they are positioned under 45 degrees. There is also a main switch. The main transformer is oil-cooled and has two secondary windings, one of each supplies one of the rectifier groups with current. Each of the two groups feed each of the two driving motors, positioned in parallel. The 2,900 KVA transformer has 28 steps on its secondary side, with 30-v tension steps, except from 0 to 1, when the difference is 350-v, because the motor tension has to be able to be regulated without steps within the range of the loading (slow-motion) speed; i.e., 0–40 m/min. The compensated driving motors are nose-suspended and output is 370 kw at 760-v per motor.

Like the converter locomotives, the rectifier locomotives have the same twin-cab arrangement as described above. Again, regenerative braking is provided, as well as ultra-short-wave remote control for loading and weighing journeys between 0.6–0.8 km/h. The electrical part was supplied by AEG and SSW, while Krauss-Maffei and Henschel supplied the mechanical parts. Similar locomotives were supplied by BBC-Mannheim.

In the years before World War I, the Henschel firm supplied Bo'-Bo' mining locomotives for open-cast work to mines in Japan and Manchuria. In addition, together with Siemens, it supplied between 1926 and 1951 27 similar locomotives to the State Electricity Board of Victoria, Australia, for its open-cast lignite workings. Gauge was 900 mm and 1,100-v D.C. was used. The locomotives had six pantographs, two in standard position and four under an angle at the sides. The 1951 locomotives weigh 60 tons and have four nose-suspended motors of 1,760 kw output. Maximum speed is 30 km/h and the starting tractive effort is about 18,000 kg.

Rack Locomotives for Open-cast Mining Works

As the inclines in open-cast mining work became steeper, more adhesive weight was needed so the locomotives could perform their duties. With an adhesive coefficient of ⅙ (required because of the mostly dirty conditions and badly laid rails), it means that one-third of the tractive effort is already wasted at 50‰ gradients. The only answer is to lessen the slope of gradients or use rack-traction. In 1939, a German mining firm ordered such rack locomotives from BBC-Mannheim. They have a tractive effort of 42,000 kg. These locomotives had the wheel-arrangement 2'4Zo'2' and weighed 90 tons. Output was 4 x 245 kw/h.

Other main dimensions were: total length, 14,076 mm; pivot distance, 9,450 mm; bogie wheel base, 2,000 mm; wheel diameter, 900 mm; 1-hour tractive effort, 38,000 kg at 8.6 km/h. A very interesting technical design followed in 1946, ordered by a German lignite mine. Two D.C. rack locomotives were ordered for 900-mm gauge.

Electric Locomotives for Industry

These locomotives fulfill the many industrial transport needs, such as movement of ore, stone, coal, liquid steel, hot coke, and ashes, either within or beyond the factory areas. All types of currents are

2'–4Zo'–2'– rack open-cast mining locomotive built in 1940 by BBC-Mannheim.

Rack open-cast mining locomotive for Fortuna mine, West Germany.

Drive and motors for rack open-cast mining locomotive.

being used, as well as voltages of 220 to 10,000. Such locomotives were built as special vehicles in the last .60 to 70 years but also in serial production, their weights varying from 8 to 100 tons. The use of battery locomotives is receding, both because of high costs and limited use as compared with overhead-supplied locomotives.

These latter vehicles are now predominant in industry and use mostly D.C. of 220–1,200-v; there are also two-power locomotives, which contain either a diesel engine or battery when running on nonelectrified lines. Output has gone up to 750 kw/h and 12,000 kg/h tractive effort, with weights of 75 tons and usually Bo'Bo' wheel arrangement. They are driven by two to four nose-suspended motors, with an average speed of 20 km/h and a maximum speed of 40 km/h.

The most interesting and important examples of industrial electric locomotives are the ones previously described for open-cast mining operations. Another example is the "coking locomotive," used to convey glowing coke from blast furnaces in steel-works to cooling towers and storage bunkers. The driver's cab is positioned as high as possible to supervise the removal of coke from the furnaces. These locomotives are often used with 3-phase A.C. current, which is taken from three current rails lying between or beside the running rails. The 3-phase A.C. slip-ring motor is fixed longitudinally between the axles and transmits power by a geardrive. There are also types driven by normal D.C. nose-suspended motors.

Another interesting example is the 600-v D.C. ore-transporter motor coach that BBC-Mannheim supplied to the Westphalia mine in Dortmund, West Germany. Two units supplied in 1957 are used for transporting iron ore from storage bunkers to the blast furnaces. They weigh 100 tons and have the wheel-arrangement (A2) (2A). Their loading space is 80 m³ with a loading capacity of 80 tons, the whole vehicle weighing 180 tons. Total length is 17,994 mm; pivot distance, 11,200 mm; bogie wheel base, 1,500 mm; wheel diameter, 940 mm; 1-hour tractive effort, 7,500 kg at 5.7 kilometers. The outer axle of

Standard gauge "coking" locomotive. Built for a steel works in Lorraine, France; 161 tons, 380-v, 3-phase A.C.

Coking locomotive and wagon during loading.

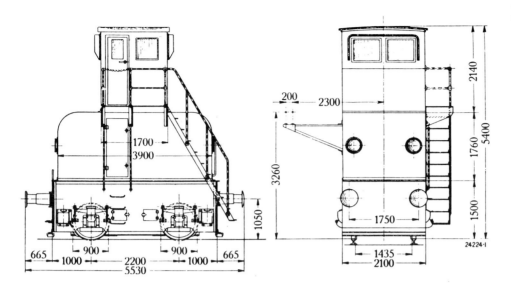

Schematic illustration of a coking locomotive.

(Ao2) (Ao2) ore-distributing motor coach for Westphalia mine, for 600-v D.C., 2 x 50 kw/1-hour, 1954.

the 3-axle bogies is motorized with an output of 2 x 50 kw/1-hour. The driver's cab is on one end. Other examples are locomotives for haulage of ships through canals and canal locks, as on the Panama Canal.

The design of electric industrial locomotives changed little between 1900 and 1960. Illustrated are a -Bo'- locomotive built by Mather and Platt in 1895–1900 and one built by Brown Boveri in 1922. The latter was destined for rack-and-adhesion service and used 550-v D.C. The locomotive weighed 12 tons and had an output of 31.5 to 51.5 km/1-hour.

In 1962, Messrs. Krupp and AEG supplied an interesting works locomotive in which all axles were coupled with the motor-drive to exploit the adhesive weight to the fullest extent and avoid slipping. The vehicle is of all-welded construction and can run both under 15,000-v, 1-phase A.C. of 16⅔ and 50 cycles.

Electric industrial shunting locomotive from Mather and Platt, England, about 1895–1900.

The motor, positioned high above the frame, drives the axles of both bogies by a seven-wheel gear drive. The locomotive is grid-controlled and thus has practically no switchgear; it also can be battery-driven to enter nonelectrified areas. Other main dimensions are: weight in working order, 80 tons; total length, 14,940 mm; bogie wheel base, 1,750 mm; wheel diameter, 1,120 mm; 1-hour tractive effort, 19,000 kg; and maximum tractive effort, 27,000 kg.

In 1965, the VEB locomotive works, Hans Beimler, in Henningsdorf near Berlin, East Germany (formerly the famous AEG factory) supplied an interesting industrial locomotive in two units to the USSR. Required were powerful locomotives to ascend gradients of 60–70‰ in open-cast mining operations. A special train was designed that consisted of the locomotive and two self-discharging wagons. The wagons are 4-axled and have each two fully motorized bogies (as has the locomotive). In addition, there is a diesel motor of 750 hp and a 450-kw generator to run on nonelectrified lines. One end of the locomotive has two cabs (left and right). The bogies are stabilized by the locomotive body. The latter has four-point suspension on each bogie. The electrical installations consist of a low-tension control unit with silicone rectifiers and two motors in parallel (per bogie). Main dimensions are in Table 15.

Table 15
RUSSIAN INDUSTRIAL LOCOMOTIVE

	Locomotive	Self-discharge Wagon
Wheel arrangement	Bo'-Bo'	Bo'-Bo'
Weight (tons)	120	65
Loading capacity (tons)	—	55
Axle load (tons)	30	30
Gauge (mm)	1,524	1,524
Length (mm)	19,900	16,200
Wheel diameter (mm)	1,120	1,120
Pivot distance (mm)	14,280	11,580
1-hour output of the 4 motors (kw)	1,640	1,640
Tractive effort (kg) at km/h	22,700/25.7	22,700/25.7
Maximum tractive effort (kg)	39,900	39,500
Maximum speed (km/h)	50	50

Works locomotive for rack-and-adhesion service built in 1922 by Brown Boveri.

Eighty-ton locomotive built for 15,000-v, 1-phase A.C. of 16⅔ or 50 Hz.

Russian industrial locomotive for use with two fully motorized self-discharge wagons for open-cast mining.

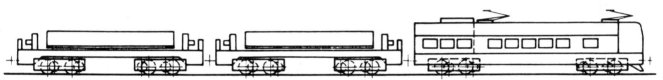

Russian industrial locomotive.

The Underground Post Office Tube Railway in London

This unique railway dating from 1927 can be considered either a "tube" line or an industrial railway because it serves exclusively postal and parcel services. The line is entirely in tunnels, has 2-foot gauge (620 mm), and eight stations. The line has two pairs of rails with four-line stations. It is about 11-km-long and is operated by a current rail with 440-v D.C. Each train consists of three wagons, each 27 feet long. Each coachbody has four containers for mailbags. The trains have no drivers but move by remote control from station to station, where they are braked automatically.

Each station has an attendant who controls loading, unloading, and starting by electromagnetic driving elements. The railway follows a strict time-table, and in its 50 years of existence has never had an accident. There is also a small motor coach for inspection and maintenance work. The line moves about 45,000 mailbags per day, the total traveling time being 18 minutes; maximum speed is 50 km/h.

London Post Office Railway.

London Post Office Railway.

Part 3   Biographies of Important Personalities of the Electric Traction System

Within the framework of a book giving a short history of electric traction, it is possible to mention only a few of the great engineers who contributed to the success of the electric railway, which celebrated its centennial in 1979.

Werner von Siemens (1816–92)

Werner von Siemens was born in 1816 in Lenthe near Dresden, Germany. He came from a large family and entered artillery school in Berlin, since he had been interested in technical subjects from an early age.

As a young officer, he had several inventions to his credit, such as a device to measure ballistic speed, as well as a production method for explosives. He also occupied himself with telegraphy and eventually joined the telegraph department of the general staff.

After the Danish war, he built the first telegraph line from Berlin to Hamburg and founded his own firm, Siemens and Halske. In 1867, Halske left the firm and Werner's brothers, Wilhelm and Friedrich, joined the firm.

Werner's major contribution was the invention

Werner von Siemens, 50 years old.

of the dynamo, which led to the first electric locomotive in 1879. In the same year, the firm founded a branch in Vienna. Two world-famous firms were developed, Siemens and Halske and Siemens-Schuckert.

Werner also was active in other fields, helping to create technical universities as well as an effective patent law. He was enobled and died at 76 in 1892. He wrote an autobiography, "Memories of Werner von Siemens."

Wilhelm Siemens (1823–83)

Wilhelm was only eight years old when his father died, and Werner helped him choose a technical career. Wilhelm was a talented and important engineer and inventor, and the life-long correspondence with his brother has survived.

As a young man, Wilhelm's attention was focused on England, where a modern industry began to develop; in 1843 he went to England, originally to exploit Werner's invention of a galvanizing process. He was only twenty years old but successfully sold the idea for 30,000 DM. In 1844, he again traveled to England, and after various unsuccessful attempts to establish himself he became, together with his brother Friedrich, Werner's agent in England.

In 1863, they built a cable-works and began to become well known in this field. Halske had left, so the firm in England was now called Siemens Brothers, the two brothers being the sole proprietors. Wilhelm had married and become a British subject. Their great success was the laying of the cable line to India for the British government.

Wilhelm was also the inventor of the famous Siemens-Martin process of steelmaking. In 1874, the firm laid the first trans-Atlantic cable. The brothers also helped to develop Werner's ideas of electric traction. In 1889, Wilhelm published his scientific efforts in three volumes. He was knighted as Sir William Siemens and died at an early age in 1883.

Frank Julian Sprague (1857–?)

Sprague was born in 1857 in Milford, Connecticut. He studied four years at the Naval Academy in Annapolis, became acquainted with Thomas Alva Edison, and started to interest himself in electrical machinery. He began a naval career but left in 1883 to work with Edison.

On a visit to London he had seen the steam-operated underground railway and had had the idea of building an electric railway with catenary and current return on running rails. After his return to the United States, he left Edison and formed, together with E. H. Johnson, the Sprague Electric Railway and Motor Company.

In the beginning, the firm supplied motors, but in 1885 Sprague proposed to Boston authorities to build an electric train with its motors positioned under the coaches and with regenerative braking. On a test line near New York, he started to try out his ideas using 600-v D.C. from a central current rail. Successful tests on the Manhattan overhead followed, but railway circles remained skeptical.

Sprague's first order came in 1887 for the newly built tram-line in Richmond, Virginia. There were, of course, a small number of electric railways in existence in Europe, but the new contract also asked for a power station, 20-kilometer catenary, and 40 motor coaches, each with 2 x 7.5-hp motors. Current was to be 450-v D.C. and was to be taken from the overhead line by pole current collectors. The motors were already of the nose-suspended type, another of his inventions. Ambitiously, Sprague had undertaken to start services in three months and was indeed able to do so. Despite the fact that the line had many curves, gradients of up to 10‰, and incorporated many novel ideas, services started in full in 1888.

Sensational success followed, Sprague receiving orders for no less than 110 railway lines. He amalgamated with Edison, then with Thompson-Houston, and finally formed what was to be the General Electric Company.

Sprague undertook similar work with lifts and elevators and was again very successful. He proposed an express line for New York with multiple-unit trains. The first such line was, however, the Chicago Elevated, which introduced in 1897 a six-coach train with multiple-unit control.

When the South Side Elevated Railroad went bankrupt in Chicago, the company was reorganize and engaged Sprague, who proposed that the company use his newly invented multiple-unit control system. The new system aroused considerable misgivings and the first vehicles were ordered in 1897 to very strict specifications. Two experimental cars were supplied that were built by the General Electric Company in Schenectady, New York. The tests were highly successful and within one year it was decided to give up locomotive haulage and use only motor coaches and trailers.

Sprague's idea was to assemble trains from several vehicles and them and their motors from one

F. J. Sprague

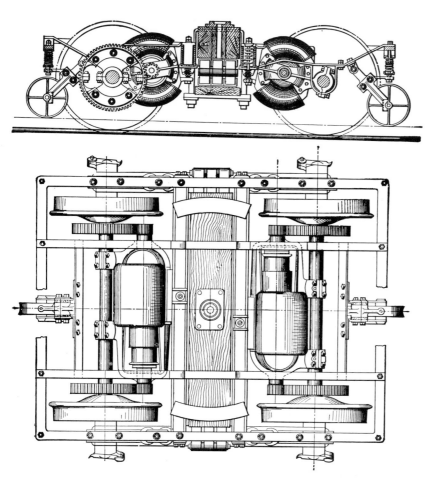

Sprague's original design of bogie and motors for the New York elevated railroad, 1885–1886.

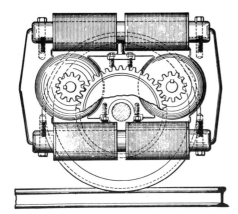

Electric motor by Sprague with twin armature—1886.

point of the train without using a locomotive. Originally, a mechanical device was tested whereby a shaft ran through the whole train, was to be coupled to the controller, and was to be moved by rotation. Sprague, however, fixed a small motor at every controller and moved these auxiliary motors from any one point of the train with an electric connection. The individual controllers at each coach were moved by compressed air. The American engineer Elihu Thompson suggested that the main controller be replaced by a series of simple switches that could be operated magnetically.

Many elevated and underground lines followed the successful Chicago Elevated. Sprague also developed an automatic multiple-unit control that was first built by Westinghouse. In 1904, this firm received the contract to supply 430 motor coaches for the so-called Interborough Rapid Transit Subway in New York. The vehicles were at that time already of all-steel construction, and in 1906 a similar contract came for the Long Island Railroad. During World War I, Sprague worked as adviser to the Marine Department and invented the twin-lift system.

William Atcheson Traill (1844–1934)

W. A. Traill was born in 1844, studied at Trinity College, Dublin, and became Master of Engineering in 1873. He worked first for the Cartographic Authority, but became interested in electric railways and developed many ideas to improve electric traction. He had the idea of the Giant Causeway Railway, and also planned the Liverpool Overhead line. He built a model of the Giant Causeway line, which was certainly the first electric model railway. It is pre-

served in the Belfast Transport Museum. He was also the first engineer to suggest the laying of the current rail between the running rails. He died in 1934 at age 90.

Michael von Dolivo-Dobrowolsky (1862–1920)

Michael von Dolivo-Dobrowolsky was born in St. Petersburg (Leningrad) in 1862. Between 1880 and 1884, he studied mechanical engineering and electrical work in Riga and Darmstadt. He entered the German Edison Company and later the AEG, one of the leading electrical firms even today. Dolivo-Dobrowolsky interested himself in Ferrari and Teslas' work on multi-phase currents and motors. In 1889 he succeeded in building a practical 3-phase motor and invented the name Drehstrom ("turning" current) for 3-phase current.

The 3-phase D.C. asynchrone motor came next, followed by Oscar von Miller's experiments in 1890–91 to transmit high-tension alternating currents over long distances—the beginning of our modern electrical supply systems. He also invented, among many other ideas, the 3-phase A.C. transformer. Dolivo-Dobrowolsky retired in 1919 and continued to work as a consultant, dying at the early age of 58 in Darmstadt.

Charles E. L. Brown (1863–1924)

C.E.L. Brown was born in 1863 in Winterthur, Switzerland. His father was an English mechanical engineer who had emigrated to Switzerland. The

W. A. Traill

Charles E. L. Brown

younger Brown trained at the Technicum in Zurich and, although only 22, took over the management of the electro-technical department of the firm of Oerlikon. He worked there for six years and developed D.C. motors, as well as generators and transformers for a 25,000-v D.C. transmission line in Germany. He also equipped the first electric locomotives in Switzerland.

Among his colleagues in Oerlikon was Walter Boveri, who came from Mannheim in Germany. In 1891, the two young engineers formed their own company, Brown, Boveri & Co., in Baden near Zurich. The young firm underwent great difficulties but was helped by the ever-increasing growth of the electrical industry. Brown worked first of all on A.C. techniques and was very active in early railway electrifications. He also invented the cylindrical rotor for turbo-generators, and the firm became the leader in single- and multiple-phase generators.

In 1912, Brown received the honorary doctorate of the university in Karlsruhe. He died in 1924 as one of the pioneers of industry who created the basis for the world-wide firm that now employs 75,000 people and produces many leading efforts, especially in electric railway engineering.

René Thury (1860–1938)

René Thury's father was part-owner of a small engineering and instrument works in Geneva, SIP. Young Thury entered the firm in 1874 and became

very interested in early electric machinery. He was obviously mechanically talented quite early on—in 1877, for example, he constructed (together with a friend) a steam-operated tricycle that reached 50 km/h.

At this time, T. A. Edison of the United States decided to set up a works in Europe and chose the small SIP firm; the purpose was to manufacture his electric lamps. Young Thury was sent to the United States to work with Edison, who soon noticed the very talented young man. When Thury returned to Geneva, lamp manufacturing was started. He also worked on the first D.C. installation in Lausanne.

Later, Thury left SIP and entered the firm of Cuénod et de Meuron, also a small factory for electrical instruments and machinery in Geneva. He soon became very successful designing some multi-pole machines for an exhibition in Zurich. The firm underwent various changes and finally, in 1918, became the S.A. des Atéliers de Sécherôn, the name of the district where the factory was located. In 1884, two years before Brown's experiments, Thury electrified the small railway Taubenloch–Waterfall–Beaujean. He succeeded in building a 50-m-long cable line with 30‰ gradient to erect near Territet/Montreux. The experiments aroused world-wide interest, and Thury began to experiment with power transmission over greater distances. He married, had six children (five daughters and one son), but continued to work ceaselessly.

He helped build the Bürgenstrock and Stanserhorn railways and invented the series-connected D.C. motor in 1890. He had little interest in financial success, so he presented his important inventions to

René Thury

his old friend and employer, Hermann Cuénod. The motors were supplied by Sécherôn for 35 years, the last one for a firm in Peru.

From 1891 onwards, Thury occupied himself mainly with problems of electric traction and power transmission. There were many successes, among them the railway on Mount Salève in 1892, the electric line Orbe–Chavornay in 1894, and many other lines all over the world. In 1900 there followed Aigle–Leysin and Bex–Villars, while in the transmission field the line to St. Meurice was erected. Then came the important high-tension and D.C. locomotives for St. George de Commiers–La Mûre.

In 1910, at 50 years old, Thury decided to leave Sécherôn and become a consulting engineer. He undertook work for famous firms like Alsthom and Dick and Kerr & Company. In his personal life, he suffered great tragedy when both his wife and son were killed in a motor accident and he also lost his right eye. In spite of this, he continued to be very active and died peacefully in 1938 at age 78. These few lines can hardly do justice to the great personality and talents of Thury.

Emil Huber-Stockar (1866–1939)

Emil Huber-Stockar was born in 1866. He studied at the Polytechnicum in Zurich and in 1888 entered the service of M. F. Oerlikon. By 1891, he was a director and remained with the firm until 1912, finally as managing director. From Oerlikon he went to the SBB and became manager of the newly created traction department.

From the start, he was the father of electric railways in Switzerland, and his life is really the history of the Swiss electric railways and their fabulous success. It was Huber-Stockar who worked out the plans for the electrification of the Gotthard line. The first World War interrupted these plans, and, after many arguments about the best system, his views prevailed. Already by 1917 it was decided to electrify the Swiss main lines—the work was to take until 1939 but was later accelerated to 1929, again following Huber-Stockar's plans.

He retired as chief engineer in 1925 and remained as consultant. In 1928, he published the well-known memorandum, "The Electrification of the SBB till 1928." He died suddenly in 1939.

Hans Behn-Escherburg (1864–1938)

Hans Behn-Escherburg was born in 1864 in Zurich, the son of a literature professor. The father died young and the son studied physics under H. F. Weber at the Technical University of Zurich. After experiments with power-transmission, he went in 1892 to Oerlikon. After Brown left this firm, a new one was formed under Huber-Stockar, which was joined by

Emil Huber-Stockar

Hans Behn-Escherburg

Behn-Escherburg. After five years he became a leading engineer and in a life of ceaseless effort became one of the leading figures of the young electrical industry.

He was one of the pioneers of the 1-phase motor for railway use. The low-frequency motor for the Seebach-Wettingen experiments of the SBB were developed by him; output of the motor was 250 hp/1-hour and 140 hp/continuous. When this system was accepted for the electrification of the Bernese Alpine Railway (the BLS), he designed the 1,000-hp and then 1,500-hp motors for the powerful locomotives needed, at that time the most powerful in the world.

When the SBB accepted the same system, Huber-Stockar became chief engineer and Behn-Escherburg technical director of Oerlikon. He occupied himself with many technical problems, including recuperative braking. He retired in 1928 but continued an active life both scientifically and literary. He died in 1938.

Friedrich Eichberg (Dates unknown)

Friedrich Eichberg began his practical training in 1902 with the Union E.G. in Vienna. From there, he went to the AEG–Berlin in 1904 and ran its railway department until 1912. Together with Winter, he created the famous Winter–Eichberg motor, considered one of the first 1-phase A.C. motors. He followed the work of Déri, Arnold, and Eickemeyer.

These motors were developed for the experiments of Prussian State Railways on the line Niederschoeneweide–Spindlersfeld (see page 4). The experiments were very satisfactory and led to electrification with 6,000-v 25 Hz 1-phase A.C. of the line Hamburg–Blankenese–Ohlsdorf (see page 63). Then came the experimental locomotives for Dessau-Bitterfeld that also were designed by Eichberg. He left the AEG in 1912 and went to Linke-Hoffmann, where he founded a new field of activity.

Ivan August Öfverholm (1874–?)

I. A. Öfverholm was born in 1874 and after studying at Stockholm he entered the firm of ASEA in Västeròs. Later he worked at General Electric in Schenectady, N.Y. In 1904 he returned, and in 1915 became director of the electrical department of the Swedish State Railways. Under his guidance, the early electrifications of the SJ were carried out and he assisted materially in the design of the new electric traction vehicles.

Friedrich Eichberg

Koloman von Kando

Koloman von Kando (1869–1931)

The firm of Ganz in Budapest and its chief engineer, Koloman von Kando, were the pioneers in the design of 3-phase A.C. traction and its motors and vehicles. His first success was the Italian Valtellina line, which was followed by many interesting designs for the Italian State Railways (until recently, electrified with 3-phase A.C.) The system of using industrial frequency was then taken up energetically by French engineers and led to the world-wide adoption of the 25,000-v industrial frequency system.

George Westinghouse (1846–1914)

George Westinghouse was born in 1846 in New York and died there in 1914, after a most successful and active life. His great-grandfather emigrated in 1755 from Westphalia to the United States. His father was an inventor and owner of a factory for agricultural machinery. After the Civil War, Westinghouse went to Union College in Schenectady, N.Y., and made his first invention to re-rail derailed freight wagons.

From 1867–69, he worked on the airbrake that carries his name and opened his own factory in Pittsburgh. The great success of his brake system led to the establishment of factories the world over. However, Westinghouse occupied himself with many other problems, such as a central coupling, which he developed for the New York underground system. Later, he turned to high-tension transmission problems, especially in power station and traction work.

At the end of his life, his factories employed over 50,000 people. He received many honors in his lifetime, such as the Edison medal.

Bibliography

(A short bibliography is attached giving some of the more important publications dealing in greater detail with the subject of electric locomotives.)

A. Books in English

Electric Locomotives, Baldwin-Westinghouse, Philadelphia and Pittsburgh, 1896.

Electric Traction, R. H. Smith, Harper Bros, New York, 1900

Electric Railways, S. Ashe & J. W. Keiley, Constable, London, 1905

Electric Traction, Sir Philip Dawson, *The Electrician*, London, 1909

Electric Traction, E. P. Burgh, McGraw-Hill, New York, 1911

Single-phase Railways, E. Austin, Constable, London, 1919

The Electric Locomotive, F. W. Carter, *Proceedings of the Institution of Civil Engineers*, 1916

Electric Traction, A. T. Dover, Pitman, London (three editions), 1917, 1929, 1954

History of the Baldwin Locomotive Works, Baldwin, Philadelphia, 1920

Electric Trains, Agnew, Virtue and Co., London, 1937

Electric Traction Jubilee, J. H. Cansdale, BTH London, 1946

Electric and Diesel-Electric Locomotives, D. W. and M. Hinde, Macmillan, London, 1947

British Electric Trains, HWA Linecar, Ian Allen, London, 1947

Individual Axle Drive, A. Hug, International Railway Congress Journal, Brussels, 1949–50

The Early History of the Electric Locomotive, F. J. G. Haut, London, 1949–51

Electricity in Transport, H. H. Andrews, English Electric Co., London, 1951

Electric Trains and Locomotives, B. K. Cooper, Leonard Hill, London, 1953

B. Books in German

Bau & Betrieb Elektr. Bahnen, M. Schliemann, O. Leiner, Leipzig, 1899

Elektr. Vollbahn-Lokomotiven, H. Zipp, O. Leiner, Leipzig, 1917

Elektr. Zugförderung, E. E. Seefehlner, Springer-Berlin (two editions), 1922 and 1924

Elektr. Lokomotiven, K. Sachs, Springer, Berlin, 1928

50 Jahre Elektrische Lokomotive, El. Bahnen, Munich, 1929

Elektrische Vollbahn-Lokomotiven, Grünholz, Norden, Berlin, 1930

Das Elektrische Eisenbahnwesen der Gegenwart, El. Bahnen, Munich, 1936

50 Jahre Elektro-Vollbahn-Lokomotiven, A. Koci, Ployer, Vienna, 1952

Elektrische Zugförderung, K. Sachs, Huber-Frauenfeld, 1953

Österreichs Lokomotiven & Triebwagen, H. Stocklausner, Ployer, Vienna, 1954

Elektrische Fahrzeugantriebe, P. Mueller, Oldenbourg, Munich, 1960

Archiv Elektrischer Lokomotiven, Bäzold & Fiebig, Transpress, Berlin, 1963

Union E.G. Berlin, Elektr. Bahnen, W. R. Reimann, Motorbuch-Verlag, Stuttgart

C. Books in French

La Traction Electrique, A. Blondel and F. P. Dubois (two volumes), Ch. Béranger, Paris, 1898

Chemins de fer Electrique, A. Bachellery, S. B. Baillière, Paris, 1923

Traction Electrique, Seefehlner & Peter, Ch. Béranger, Paris, 1926

La Commande Individuelle, A. Hug, Birkhäuser, Basel, 1931–3

Histoire de la Traction Electrique, Y. Machefart-Tessin, (two volumes) Paris, 1980

La Vie Du Rail—Traction Electrique (Special Issue, No 313), Paris ca., 1951

La Traction Electrique, G. A. Garreau, Ribea, Paris, 1965

D. Periodicals

Engineering (especially between 1880–1910), London

Journal of the Institution of Locomotive Engineers, London

Elektrische Bahnen, Munich

La Vie du Rail, Paris

The Locomotive (from 1897 onwards), London

Electric Railway Traction Supplement of the Railway Gazette, London

*Journals of the Institution of Civil, Mechanical and Electrical
    Engineers*, London
International Railway Congress Bulletin, Brussels
Railway Age, Philadelphia
Railway Gazette, London
The Railway Engineer, London

E. Reports of Committees, Congresses, etc.
'Bericht der Schweizerischen Studienkommission für El.
    Bahnbetrieb', Wyssling, Rascher, Zurich, 1912–14
London Brighton and South Coast Railway', Report by
    Sir Philip Dawson on the 'Proposed Substitution of Electric
    for Steam Operation for Suburban, Local and Main Line
    Passenger and Freight Services', 1921
Pringle Report', H. M. Stationery Office, London, 1927
Weir Report', H. M. Stationery Office, London, 1931
Convention on Electric Railway Traction', Institution of
    Electrical Engineers, London, March 1950
Congress on 50 cycle 1-phase a.c. Traction', Annecy, 1951
British Railways Electrification Conference', London, 1960
Conference on Euston Main Line Electrification', British
    Railways, London, October 1966

Index